The Music
Library

The History
of Reggae

Other books in this series include:

The History of Country Music
The History of Gospel Music
The History of Jazz
The History of Rock and Roll
The History of the Blues

The Music Library

The History of Reggae

by Stuart A. Kallen

LUCENT BOOKS
An imprint of Thomson Gale, a part of The Thomson Corporation

Detroit • New York • San Francisco • San Diego • New Haven, Conn. • Waterville, Maine • London • Munich

LIBRARY OF CONGRESS CATALOGING-IN-PUBLICATION DATA

Kallen, Stuart A., 1955–
  The history of reggae / by Stuart A. Kallen.
    p. cm. — (The music library)
  Includes bibliographical references and index.
  ISBN 1-59018-740-7 (hard cover : alk. paper)
  1. Reggae music—History and criticism—Juvenile literatue. I. Title. II. Series: Music library (San Diego, Calif.)
ML3532.K35 2005
781.646'09—dc22
                                         2005008789

Printed in the United States of America

• Contents •

•Foreword•

In the nineteenth century English novelist Charles Kingsley wrote, "Music speaks straight to our hearts and spirits, to the very core and root of our souls. . . . Music soothes us, stirs us up . . . melts us to tears." As Kingsley stated, music is much more than just a pleasant arrangement of sounds. It is the resonance of emotion, a joyful noise, a human endeavor that can soothe the spirit or excite the soul. Musicians can also imitate the expressive palate of the earth, from the violent fury of a hurricane to the gentle flow of a babbling brook.

The word music is derived from the fabled Greek muses, the children of Apollo who ruled the realms of inspiration and imagination. Composers have long called upon the muses for help and insight. Music is not merely the result of emotions and pleasurable sensations, however.

Music is a discipline subject to formal study and analysis. It involves the juxtaposition of creative elements such as rhythm, melody, and harmony with intellectual aspects of composition, theory, and instrumentation. Like painters mixing red, blue, and yellow into thousands of colors, musicians blend these various elements to create classical symphonies, jazz improvisations, country ballads, and rock-and-roll tunes.

Throughout centuries of musical history, individual musical elements have been blended and modified in infinite ways. The resulting sounds may convey a whole range of moods, emotions, reactions, and messages. Music, then, is both an expression and reflection of human experience and emotion.

The foundations of modern musical styles were laid down by the first ancient musicians who used wood, rocks, animal skins—and their own bodies—to recreate the sounds of the natural world in which they lived. With their hands, their feet, and their very breath they ignited the passions of listeners and moved them to their feet. The dancing, in turn, had a mesmerizing and hypnotic effect that allowed people to transcend their worldly concerns. Through music they could achieve a level of shared experience that could not be found in other forms of communication. For this reason, music has always been part of religious endeavors, from ancient Egyptian religious ceremonies to modern Christian masses. And it has inspired dance movements from kings and queens spinning the minuet to punk rockers slamming together in a mosh pit.

By examining musical genres ranging from Western classical music to rock and roll, readers will find a new understanding of old music and develop an appreciation for new sounds. Books in Lucent's Music Library focus on the music, the musicians, the instruments, and on music's place in cultural history. The songs and artists examined may be easily found in the CD and sheet music collections of local libraries so that readers may study and enjoy the music covered in the books. Informative sidebars, annotated bibliographies, and complete indexes highlight the text in each volume and provide young readers with many opportunities for further discussion and research.

Introduction

The Movement of the People

Reggae is international music that is popular on every continent. The music has been adopted and stylized to fit local tastes by musicians all over the world. Whether the music is heard in Tokyo or Texas, the roots of reggae remain in Jamaica, an island nation in the Caribbean that is home to 3 million people. Although the music emanates from a tiny island, its popularity is testimony to its power, according to music journalist Lloyd Bradley writing in *Reggae: The Story of Jamaican Music*:

> Given that Jamaica is an otherwise relatively insignificant island in the Caribbean, with a population half the size of London's and just about every post-colonial problem on the dial, that its music should have such an impact on the rest of the planet is remarkable. Then, when you take into account that a mere forty-five years ago, Jamaican popular music, or any modern indige-

nous cultural expression, simply did not exist, reggae's story is little short of astonishing.[1]

Because of its great popularity, reggae is Jamaica's main cultural export and one that identifies the country for most people living elsewhere. Outsiders who love reggae appreciate the music for its danceable beat, the reggae rhythms, or "riddims" as they say in Jamaica. To the people of the island, however, reggae lyrics are no less important, for the best songs blend elements of history, protest, deep spirituality, celebration of daily joys of life in the tropics, and commentary on the realities of life, crime, poverty, and despair in an underdeveloped nation. To native Jamaicans, the music represents African roots that go back over four centuries to the days when black slaves were brought to the island to work the sugarcane plantations. Although the European slave masters tried to impose their religious and secular music on the slaves, the Africans retained many traditions of the music and dance of their native cultures. They took the parts of white music that appealed to them and fused them with the rhythms and tonal scales of their homeland. This music provided a source of strength to the oppressed people, whose survival remains dependent on hard work such as walking long distances to gather food. As reggae musician Rupie Edwards explains:

> This is music that's come down from slavery, through colonialism, so it's more than just a style. If you're coming from the potato walk or the banana walk on the hillside, people sing. To get rid of their frustrations and lift the spirits, people sing. It was also your form of entertainment at the weekend, whether in church or at a [club] or just outside a your house, you was going to sing. If you're cutting down a bush you're gonna sing, if you're digging some ground you're gonna sing. The music is vibrant. It's a way of life, the whole thing is

The harshness of life for most Jamaicans, like these photographed in a Kingston slum in 1964, is a common theme of reggae music.

not just a music [that's] been made, it's a people . . . culture . . . it's an attitude, it's a way of life coming out of a people.[2]

Over the centuries, this way of life included slavery, prejudice, economic discrimination, and injustice. Living conditions where reggae developed, in the Trench Town slums of the capital city of Kingston, are notoriously harsh. In the ghettos, called shantytowns, people live in shacks made from scraps of wood and corrugated tin, with no running water or electricity. Daily life is dominated by the stench of open sewers, the hopelessness of rampant unemployment, and the brutality of rival gangs. In this environment it is little wonder that songwriters sing about single mothers raising children, young men behind prison bars, gang violence, and racial tensions. Others celebrate those who rebel, violent heroes called "rude boys," who provoke clashes with authorities, steal from the rich, fight the oppressive police, and help the poor. As reggae artist Linton Kwesi Johnson states:

> The sounds of reggae . . . are the sounds of screeching [tires], bottles breaking, wailing sirens, gunfire, people screaming and shouting, children crying. They are the sounds of apocalyptic thunder and earthquakes; of chaos and curfew. The sounds of reggae are the sounds of a society in the process of transformation, a society undergoing political and historical change.[3]

Not all reggae is a product of street culture, however. Lyricists often use biblical elements to uplift their listeners, singing of a promised land in the context of a philosophy of peace and unity. In her "Jamaican Patois and the Power of Language in Reggae Music" Web article, Stacey Herbold decodes some biblical terms used in reggae lyrics:

> Reggae musicians . . . consider "Babylon" the corrupt establishment of the 'system,' Church and State . . . the police. . . . "Zion" is the opposite of "Babylon." It represents a place of freedom and equality. . . . Jehovah or "Jah" is . . . God, who is considered the past emperor of Ethiopia. . . . "Jah" symbolizes love, power, goodness, and protection.[4]

Different Styles

As a vehicle of hope and protest, the traditional, or "roots," reggae style emerged from earlier genres, such as ska, with similar lyrical content. After Bob Marley popularized roots reggae in the late 1970s, the music continued to change, spawning new reggae styles known as dancehall and ragga. These genres incorporate political topics and more typical dancehall concerns such as sex, fashion, and the latest dance steps. Together reggae and its offshoots, performed and marketed everywhere, generate much-needed income back in Jamaica. In an average year, the Jamaican recording industry brings in $300 million in sales in the United States alone.

Bob Marley performs in London in 1980. More than two decades after his death, music lovers still equate Marley with roots reggae.

In addition, the music has come to influence world culture, as Larry Rother wrote in the *New York Times* in 1998:

> Every musical style to emerge from Jamaica over the last 35 years has eventually achieved international popularity. Reggae is part of the vocabulary of every working pop musician. The disc jockeys known as toasters are now acknowledged as the earliest progenitors of rap, and ska has lately become the favorite of skateboarders and punk bands the world over.[5]

Reggae has also been fused with rock and roll in songs by some of the top artists, including Sting, the Grateful Dead, Eric Clapton, the Rolling Stones, and many others.

Jamaican-style reggae has also been adapted and transformed by various cultures. In Hawaii, Jawaiian music explores issues of indigenous Hawaiians while blending reggae with traditional music, rock, and jazz. In Canada, poet Lillian Allen uses reggae riddims to sing about women's issues such as gender equality, sexual abuse, and even childbirth. In Nicaragua, the Soul Vibrations use reggae as a vehicle to protest government policies and promote revolutionary political activities. The story is the same in Africa, Mexico, and elsewhere.

From its humble roots in the Jamaican countryside and in the ghettos of Kingston, reggae has made an impact comparable to rock and roll. Whether used as an expression of protest or joy, reggae has traveled around the world in a few decades. As the music's riddims bounce between continents, picking up different interpretations wherever they are played, reggae continues to inspire musicians, dancers, and listeners and shine a musical light on an often dark world.

Chapter One

The Roots of Reggae

Modern reggae music can trace its roots back through Jamaica's long and tumultuous history, beginning in 1495 when Christopher Columbus landed on the island and declared it property of Spain. The Spanish exterminated the native Taino Indians with slavery, disease, and war, and began importing African slaves to the island in 1517. By the time the British expelled the Spanish and took formal control of Jamaica in 1670, slavery was well established. Ninety percent of the island's inhabitants could trace their heritage to central or western Africa. The other 10 percent were Scottish and English overseers, who ran huge sugar plantations that covered most of the island's coastal regions.

The tiny minority of white residents lived in constant dread of slave insurrections, which occurred on an average of once every ten years. These fears were considerably heightened during music and dance performances based on African traditions. One of the most frightening to the white population was the traditional West African fertility ritual known as Jonkanoo, translated by the British into "John Cannu." Around Christmastime, singers and dancers paraded through towns dressed in masks, beads, and colorful outfits, exhibiting bawdy and outrageous behavior. In 1774, English author Edward Long described the spectacle of a Jonkanoo celebration:

> [During the] Christmas holidays, they had several tall robust fellows dressed up in grotesque habits, and a pair of ox-horns on their head, sprouting from the top of a horrid sort of vizor, or mask, which about the mouth is rendered very [terrifying] with large boar-tusks. The masquerader, carrying a wooden sword in his hand, is followed with a numerous [crowd] of drunken women, who refresh him frequently with a [sip] of [alcoholic] aniseed-water, whilst he

An illustration shows traders bargaining over a slave. Reggae music has its roots in the African slave trade to Jamaica.

dances at every door, bellowing out John Cannu! with great vehemence; so that, what with the liquid and the exercise, most of them are thrown into dangerous fevers.[6]

Such ceremonies emboldened Jamaica's slaves and thousands of them ran away to the mountainous interior of the island, where the British were unable to control them. The runaways were known as Maroons from the Spanish word *cimarron* meaning "wild or untamed." They lived independently and fiercely resisted the British colonial system with guerrilla fighters who fostered a sense of permanent revolt among slaves.

The Maroons developed a distinctive culture that was a mix of African and European languages, religious beliefs, and customs. The rebellious Maroons provided inspiration for many of the island's later residents, including the Rastafarians, a uniquely Jamaican religious movement whose members over the years have included many reggae musicians, perhaps most famously, the legendary Bob Marley, who died in 1981.

African Traditions

African-style drums provided the musical basis for both Maroon and slave ceremonies. The *ebo* drum was made from a hollow log with a sheepskin head stretched over a hole. The bass drum, or *kyando*, was constructed from the wood of a breadfruit tree. The "talking" drum, however, was the favored drum of the black population. The drum, still in use today, is called a *burru*. It is made to "talk" by the drummer, who holds it under one arm and squeezes cords running between drumheads attached to each end of the instrument. The squeezing changes the pitch of the drum as the drummer hits the head with a curved stick. The sound is described by Chris Salewicz in *Reggae Explosion: The Story of Jamaican Music* as "magical, machine-gun like clatters and sighing spaces."[7]

The burru was originally used to pace slaves working in the fields, as Jamaican ethnomusicologist Verena Reckord writes: "It was one of the few forms of African music allowed by slave masters because of its function as a 'work metronome' for the slaves. Burru bands were allowed in the fields to play the music that buoyed the spirits of the slaves and make them work faster and so speed up production."[8]

Burru drummers were often unemployed, however, as workers were not in the fields every day. During times of no work, the drummers gathered in the poorer neighborhoods of Kingston to practice songs and perform. In the nineteenth century, the burru drummers developed their own lyrical style that can also be traced back to traditional African origins, as Reckord explains:

Burru songs closely parallel the "praise songs" of original African tradition, which would expose the good or evil aspects of a person or a village. . . . [The] Burru people sang topical songs about current events and especially about "newsmakers" in the community who, during the year, may have been guilty of some misconduct. This reflects another African custom found among Gold Coast tribes [of West Africa], whereby, at the end of the old year, [people] of the community would go from house to house singing derogatory songs (without calling names) about persons who had committed wrongs during the year. The accused were not allowed to retaliate directly but were free, after the musicians were through, to sing songs in their own defense. It was a sort of purification rite that absolved the village of its sins before it entered the new year. It could be more than a coincidence, therefore, that Burru musicians in Jamaica went around "singing on people" during Christmas time.[9]

The lyrical tradition perpetuated by the burru musicians remains central to Jamaican music even in modern times. Whether or not they are aware of it, deejays who "toast," or rap over instrumental rhythm tracks, are following the customs of long-ago burru and other African songsters.

Instruments from Many Cultures

Rattles and other percussive instruments also played an important part in early Jamaican music. For example, a rattle known as a *shaka* or *shake* was made from the jawbone of a horse in which the teeth had been loosened. The instrument was played by dragging a stick across the rattling teeth.

An instrument that combines percussion with musical notes is called a rumba box, or rhumba box, and is related to the African *zanza*. Players of this instrument use their fingers and thumbs to rhythmically vibrate four large pieces of metal tuned to low notes. It is described by innovative Jamaican drummer Lloyd Knibb: "Sometimes is three or four blades in the hole [in] the box. Is a box like a [beer case], but it have a hole in the middle and four steel blades. . . . like . . . the steel [bands] they put around a barrel. Well, they cut those and use those for the different bass notes."[10]

Wind instruments were also used in various ways. The Coramantee flute, made from a long black reed that produces a mournful sound, is played with the nose. The conch shell is blown to announce meetings, begin celebrations, and simply for pleasure. The loud, bellowing cow horn, made from the horn of a bull and called an *abeng*, was used for several purposes. These horns could be heard across great distances in the Jamaican Blue Mountains. They held a formal role in spiritual ceremonies, and they were also used as important tools of communication. A talented abeng blower, or "hornman," was held in high esteem in Maroon culture for his sophisticated musical vocabulary, which consisted of various toots and tones. These tones could be used to summon a distant individual by name. The hornman also used his instrument to inform faraway villages that the British were approaching and to tell the residents the exact number of soldiers, the weapons they were carrying, and the routes they were taking.

The hornman remains one of the most important symbols of Maroon identity today, and young men continue to compete to become the best abeng players. Abengs are blown to announce a death, inform the community of a body coming home to be buried, and declare the commencement of a funeral. And while

Jamaican Patois

In addition to English, people in Jamaica speak a unique language, or patois, known as Jamaican Creole, a combination of African and English. In her "Jamaican Patois and the Power of Language in Reggae Music" Web article, Stacey Herbold explains Jamaican Creole:

In Jamaica the African slaves were thrown into a situation where the only common means of communication was English, or at least broken English, therefore Jamaican Creole has a majority of its roots in English. Essential words which people could not find an English name for, such as people, things (like plants and animals) and activities (especially religious ones) were taken from a variety of West African languages. . . . Today in Jamaica, Jamaican patois falls at one extreme of the linguistic spectrum while Standard English lies at the other end of the spectrum. . . . At one end there is the educated model spoken by the elite, which follows the "London Standard." At the other extreme is what linguists call "creolized" English, fragmented English speech and syntax developed during the days of slavery with African influences. This is the speech of the peasant or laborer with little education. In the middle of the language scale there is the inclusion of Jamaican rhythm and intonation of words, which evolved within, the country calls this "Jamaicanism." . . .

The following phrases, used by Jamaicans today, are labeled "patois" by linguists. Many Jamaicans term them "Real English" [or] "Jamaican Talk":

"A fe me cyar." Translation: "It's my car."

"Mi a—go lef today." Translation: "I am [going] leaving today". . . .

"Bwaay! Mi ded tink de test was eazy." Translation: "Boy! I thought that test would [be] easy."

British soldiers are no longer a problem, abengs are blown to warn others when Jamaican police are approaching to raid the marijuana fields cultivated near most Maroon communities.

Stringed instruments, particularly the banjo, or "strum-strum," were also played by Maroons and other Jamaicans. This ancient instrument, with roots in Africa, was originally made from a large gourd, called a calabash, that was sliced in half. A piece of goatskin shaped like a drumhead was stretched tightly across the open gourd, and a long stick served as the instrument's neck. Four strings were made from rolled animal sinew. In later years, modern banjos made from wood and steel remained popular in Jamaica, as Knibb explains: "We used to use banjo . . . cause we never used to

In 2003 a Maroon man blows an abeng during a celebration to commemorate a Maroon victory over the British in 1738.

Rhythm of Africa, Melody of Europe

Although the majority of Jamaicans trace their heritage back to Africa, the European quadrille is well liked by the island's natives. Kevin O'Brien Chang and Wayne Chen explain quadrille music in Reggae Routes:

Jamaican popular music has always mixed "the rhythm of Africa and the melody of Europe." For all their obvious differences, African and European music have much in common, certainly more than either has with, say, Oriental music. And the first widespread native song form was dubbed quadrille. Quadrille in Jamaica probably originated like Bluegrass music in America, with black country ensembles trying to reproduce the stylish European dance music of the mid-nineteenth century such as the French quadrille, the Scottish reel, the waltz and polka. Four distinctive types of quadrille dances seem to have developed —the formal "Ballroom" in urban Kingston and St Andrew, the robust "camp style" in rural St Andrew and Portland, the intricate "virtuoso" in Clarendon . . . and the "Scottish reel" in the west. . . . [Probably] the earliest music Bob Marley ever heard was his great uncle's band playing quadrille tunes based on native Jamaican melodies. . . . Quadrille song and dance groups are still part of official national heritage festivals in which both children and adults take part. The usual quadrille group today has two guitars, a fife and a four-stringed banjo, with a fiddle and rumba box being added for special occasions.

have electric [power] in Jamaica [for] electric guitar . . . we used to haffe use a banjo. When you're going to the country to play, you haffe use a banjo, you can't use a [non-electric] guitar, cause a guitar is not loud enough, cause you don't have no [microphone], no electricity."[11]

While making the best use of traditional instruments, Jamaican musicians also used elements of African harmony and melody. For example, traditional African music is based on a five-note scale as opposed to the seven-note scale used in the West. Jamaican music based on the five-note scale has a moody, minor-key sound even in modern reggae.

While using African scales to play Western music, Jamaicans also adopted musical instruments from Europe, including the high-pitched flute, or fife, and the violin. In the eighteenth century, at the behest of their overseers, slaves played fiddles, fifes, drums, and occasionally banjos or guitars. These were used as musical accompaniment for the quadrille, a fast dance that originated in France and became popular in Scotland as well. When playing for their own pleasure, Jamaican musicians blended quadrille music with European military march tempos and complex African rhythms. This synthesized blend of music was so popular that quadrille bands remained active in Jamaica until the post–World War II years.

"People Getting Sweet"

On August 1, 1838, the British Parliament abolished slavery and emancipated three hundred thousand slaves in Jamaica. Without free labor, the plantation system collapsed, forcing the British to bring in very low-paid workers from China, Syria, and even Nepal to tend and harvest sugarcane. These immigrants further colored the island's culture, religion, and music, but none so much as about ten thousand "free Africans" who moved from West Africa to Jamaica between 1841 and 1865. The new arrivals introduced drumming rhythms that would later become characteristic of reggae.

These African workers, though converts to Christianity, kept their original culture alive by incorporating traditional African elements into their adopted religion. In the mid–nineteenth century Jamaica experienced an upsurge in religious activity known as the Great Revival. Two of the most popular religious sects at the time were known as Revival Zion and Pocomania, or Pukumina. Church services for both sects were filled with music that was a combination of European and African elements. While musicians played various drums, cymbals, and rattles, worshippers clapped hands, swayed, sang, jumped, and stamped and tapped their feet.

Like other elements of early Jamaican music, these sounds made their way onto records in the 1960s. For example, producer Lee "Scratch" Perry was inspired to use Pocomania elements on the 1968 hit "People Funny Boy." Speaking in light Jamaican patois, Perry describes the moment in his biography *People Funny Boy* by David Katz:

> [One] night me walking past a Pocomania church and hear the people inside a wail. And me catch the vibration and say boy! Let's make a sound [to] catch the vibration of them people! Them was in spirit and them tune me in spiritually. That's where the whole thing come from, 'cause them Poco people getting sweet.[12]

Musical Stew

African immigrants influenced religion and culture on the island while working at jobs formerly performed by Jamaicans. Even as this was occurring, thousands of Jamaicans left their home-

The religious music and rhythms of Pocomania inspired many Jamaican musicians of the 1960s, including Lee "Scratch" Perry.

land to seek work in Panama, Nicaragua, Costa Rica, Cuba, and Trinidad. In the Latin American nations, Jamaican musicians were influenced by tango and samba music, styles based on traditional African polyrhythms where drummers use several different rhythms and beats that weave and intertwine with each other. In Trinidad, calypso music, which is built around a heavy central beat, was readily adopted by Jamaicans.

Calypso, like burru, is characterized by improvised bawdy and satirical lyrics that touch on topical or humorous subjects. In the twentieth century itinerant Jamaican street singers followed this ancient tradition by improvising songs about news events and

sold the lyrics to listeners. Two of the most popular street singers, who influenced many Jamaican musicians, were Slim Beckford and Sam Blackwood. Nineteen-fifties Jamaican recording artist Noel "Skully" Simms recalls the men: "Slim and Sam were the two men who start music in Jamaica on the streetside of Spanish Town Road . . . one playing guitar and both of them sing in harmony. The songs they sing, they have it on paper, printed out, and sell it for a penny—that was their livelihood for years."[13]

As the musical influences of other nations seeped back to Jamaica, another unique brand of Jamaican music, called mento, was born. Fused with quadrille, tango, samba, and calypso, mento's many influences could be described as a musical stew, flavored with dozens of spices. Mento, which was very popular from the late nineteenth century to the 1930s, was well loved in rural areas, as Kevin O'Brien Chang and Wayne Chen explain in *Reggae Routes:*

> Even now mento is regarded ambivalently as "country" music, somewhat crude and unsophisticated but hearkening back to days of lost, rustic innocence. Like most folk music, mento was a blend of music and dance, with songs mixing narrative and topical commentary. Mento has a clear, strong fourth beat in [a four-beat measure] and closely follows local speech patterns.[14]

As the favored music of the rural poor, mento was often played on improvised instruments made from whatever scrap materials were available. Players fashioned flutes from bamboo, drums from calabashes, rattles from gourds filled with seeds, and even drums, rattles, and flutes from pieces of plastic PVC pipe. More sophisticated mento bands utilized an instrumental lineup similar to quadrille bands, featuring hand drums, rattles, fifes, banjos, and, on occasion, the rumba box.

Mento is often called Jamaican calypso. While this is not completely accurate, the names of early bands did little to discourage that description. For example, in the 1950s, the most popular mento bands were Lord Messam & the Calypsonians, Count Lasher's Calypso Quartet, and Reynold's Calypso Clippers. Mento and calypso do have similar lyrical traditions, as Steve Barrow and Peter Dalton write in *The Rough Guide to Reggae*: "Most mento songs were wryly humorous accounts of everyday life among the Jamaican poor, with plenty of references to the perennial topic of sex. Their tales of hardship and risqué descriptions of intimate acts can be seen as anticipating the preoccupations of reggae."[15]

The popularity of mento began to wane in the 1930s as increasing numbers of country people began migrating to the city to escape the hardships of rural life. As Chang and Chen write: "Young migrants attracted to the bright lights of big city Kingston associated mento with the harsh deprivations of farm life."[16] By the 1960s, the few mento bands still playing could be found performing on cruise-ship docks and beneath the balconies of tourist hotels, hoping listeners would throw money to the musicians. Jamaican singer Laurel Aitken recalls the situation: "I used to work with the Jamaican Tourist Board, welcoming people with a big broad hat on the wharf when the ships come in, singing calypsos: 'Welcome to Jamaica,' 'Jamaica Farewell,' 'Coconut Woman,' and they fling money [at] me."[17]

Homegrown Records

While the popularity of mento slowly faded over the decades, the style's contribution to Jamaican music cannot be underestimated. In the early 1950s, even

Jamaican singer Laurel Aitken began his career in the 1960s performing calypso music for tourists on cruise-ship docks.

as the music was losing popularity, several Jamaican businessmen set up studios to capitalize on the style. The first was entrepreneur Stanley Motta, who owned a chain of electrical appliance stores in Jamaica. In 1951 Motta recorded Harold Richardson and the Ticklers playing the mento songs "Don't Fence Her In" and "Glamour Girl."

At the time, there were no record manufacturing, or "pressing," facilities, in Jamaica, so the master tapes of the song were sent to Emil Shallit, owner of the Melodisc label in London, who took care of the pressing. Months later, the finished records, along with the printed labels and record sleeves, were sent back to Kingston. In the summer of 1952, the first mento ten-inch vinyl discs, made for playing on old-style record players at 78 rpm, were released in Jamaica on the MRS (Motta Recording Studio) label. Subsequent mento releases on MRS followed the same pattern; they were custom pressed in London, then shipped back for release in Jamaica.

Radio Jamaica

In the United States nearly everyone had access to radios by the end of the 1920s, but radio in Jamaica was nearly nonexistent until the mid-1950s. For example, in 1950 the population of the island was 1.3 million, but there were only twenty-three thousand radios. Things began to change when the first commercial broadcasting company, Radio Jamaica and Rediffusion (RJR), came on the air in 1950. Around the same time, cheap radios were introduced to the island, and by 1956 about six hundred thousand Jamaicans were estimated to be listening to the station. Although RJR did not play local music, its most popular show, *Calypso Corner*, did reflect the taste of listeners. Deejays on other shows, such as *Treasure Island Time* and *Sebastian Time*, played the latest records. The rest of the programming, however, consisted of bland orchestral music, country and western, and tame "Top 40" hits imported from the United States.

This led to the incongruous situation of future Jamaican stars being raised listening to American country music, as renowned reggae bass player Robbie Shakespeare recalls in *Reggae Routes*: "When I was young I listened to country and western . . . a lot: at first all you could get in Jamaica was one radio station, and that's what they played. . . . Jamaicans love sad music, music that makes us want to cry. So the singers with feeling were the ones we liked when we were growing up, everyone from Marty Robbins to Frankie Laine. . . ."

Those unhappy with local programming could tune in powerful radio stations from the southern United States on clear nights, when reception was good. Islanders listened to country music out of Nashville and rhythm-and-blues broadcasts from Miami and New Orleans.

Jamaican children gather around a radio at a Kingston school in this 1920s photo.

Motta tried to sell the records of "Don't Fence Her In" and "Glamour Girl" in the United States and Great Britain, where calypso records had become a fad, but sales were disappointing. However, when the song was played on the island radio station RJR (Radio Jamaica and Rediffusion), Jamaicans took pride in their homegrown style and snapped up the records.

As a shop owner, Motta was able to sell his records in his stores. In one shop he set up a recording studio in a back room where he had a piano, a microphone, and some primitive recording equipment. Using this studio, the producer continued to record, releasing a series of mento songs by groups such as Lord Fly, Lord Composer and His Silver Seas Hotel Orchestra, and the Calypso Clippers. It was difficult for Motta to make a profit with his studio, however, as the cost of pressing records in London was very expensive.

Around the same time as Motta's first mento hit, record producer Ken Khouri was inspired to start his own record label. In *Solid Foundation: An Oral History of Reggae* by David Katz, Khouri describes his entry into the business: "It happened by accident in Miami: I took my father there for his illness but I met someone who was selling a recording machine—a disk recorder; I bought it and came back to Jamaica. I used to go around recording calypsos at different night clubs; the first recording was with Lord Flea, 'Where Did The Little Flea Go?'"[18]

Khouri built his own studio with the help of his wife, Gloria. With only one microphone, he recorded calypso songs such as "Girl and Boy," and "Gimme More," and "Ten Penny Nail" by Hubert Porter. He distributed them on his Times Records label, selling the 78s through the Times variety store in downtown Kingston. Unhappy with the expense of having his records pressed in London, Khouri traveled to California in 1954 and purchased equipment to set up the first record-pressing plant in Kingston. He soon established the Federal label, the first sophisticated recording studio in the country.

As Khouri, Motta, and other producers released song after song, mento musicians such as Sugar Belly, Lord Flea, Lord Composer, and Lord Fly, who were once famous for their live performances, became radio stars. A new generation of Jamaicans, with near-universal access to radio, were inspired by the mento radio revolution. In the following decades, traces of mento would surface in releases by country reggae groups such as the Maytones, Stanley & The Turbines, and The Starlights. The roots reggae of the 1970s was also influenced by mento, as was the digital reggae, or "ragga," first recorded in the late 1980s. Even in the twenty-first century, the acoustic rhythms and humorous lyrics first recorded by Motta continue to influence those using the latest advances in digital technology.

Jamaican Jazz

If mento was the music of country people, Jamaica's more sophisticated citizens preferred music imported from the

Already famous in Jamaica for his animated live performances, Lord Flea became a radio star during the mento radio revolution of the 1950s.

United States. Beginning in the late 1930s and extending into the 1950s, big band jazz, with its roots in New Orleans, Chicago, Kansas City, and New York City, was part of a thriving jazz scene in Jamaica. As club owner Winston Blake recalls: "Big band, that music was also our pop music here. . . . That was the swing era, big band era: Count Basie, Tommy Dorsey, Stan Kenton, Glenn Miller. The formative bands in Jamaica played that music as dance music."[19]

Jamaican musicians added their unique flavor to American big band jazz. Orchestras such as the Arawaks changed the music to fit local tastes. They wrote their own compositions and added the Caribbean rhythms of calypso and merengue (a rapid ballroom dance that originated on Hispaniola, the island shared by Haiti and the Dominican Republic). This music, however, was mainly heard in expensive tourist hotels and high-class clubs of Kingston's wealthier neighborhoods. Few of the island's average citizens could enter such places unless employed as waiters or cooks. However, the bands served as training grounds for many future reggae musicians. For example, five men who would later be members of the ska band the Skatalites were in the popular Eric Deans Orchestra. Other big band musicians and conductors later went on to work behind the scenes in the Jamaican recording industry either as producers or session musicians who backed early reggae artists.

Big band jazz, like quadrille, calypso, and other musical styles, was transformed in Jamaica's rich musical culture. Throughout the early years, these sounds were heard only by those living in Jamaica or visiting the island. However, the existence of homegrown music instilled pride in generations of Jamaicans. And it laid the groundwork for the reggae explosion that would someday put Jamaican music on the map.

Chapter Two

The Sounds of Sound System

A Jamaican man on a Kingston street blasts music from an enormous sound system.

In the early 1950s, technology and economics produced a sound uniquely Jamaican that swept across the island at lightning speed. Known as "sound system," the music did not begin as a style, but rather as a way of playing it. The first sound systems consisted of single turntables that played 78 rpm records through amplifiers that broadcast the sound through tinny loudspeakers. By the mid-1950s, however, custom-built sound systems increased in power, volume, and technical complexity, as Salewicz explains: "Sound systems were like portable discos for giants: eventually they would consist of up to thirty or forty speakers, each as large as four or six [large suitcases] stuck together, joined by a vast, intricate pattern of cables that seemed to be an organic growth from Jamaica's profusion of dangling liana vines."[20] Each speaker cabinet, known as a "house of joy," blasted music at tooth-rattling volumes that inevitably lured crowds from miles around.

Flopping the Competition

Sound system operators were in fierce competition with one another. Those with the loudest speakers— and the best records—tried to ruin the dances of, or "flop," the competition. In The Rough Guide to Reggae *early sound system proprietor King Edwards describes his efforts to stay on top:*

I . . . bought an amplifier and many records [in the United States]. But when I came to Jamaica, I discovered that the typical sound system that they have in America was not suited to the type of dance they have here. People in Jamaica need to have a sound with a heavy bass. So I had to rebuild. I started off with a fifty-watt amplifier, made with seven or eight tubes. The first night I played . . . I was flopped. I had to regroup myself and build a bigger sound. . . .

During that period, I have to do a lot of traveling to seek top-class records—rhythm and blues music —so as to stay on top. I [realize] that when you import records, you get more bad than good ones. So I decide that the best thing is to go and select them myself. From 1958, I started to ride the plane like a bus. And I find myself in most of the states south of Washington. In the West I went to California. I went to Chicago. Because of that effort, I was able to introduce top-class records that hadn't been available in Jamaica before.

In the beginning, the music that fueled the sound system phenomenon was rhythm and blues (R&B) by Americans such as Fats Domino, Johnny Ace, Clyde McPhatter, the Platters, and Brooke Benton. Records by these artists were brought to the island by Jamaicans who had traveled to the United States to work. Since people could not hear these latest R&B tracks on the bland radio programs broadcast on RJR, sound system dances became extremely popular. The dance parties were particularly attractive to the island's poor, who could not afford to own record players. While a record player might cost an American less than 5 percent of his or her yearly income, the same device cost about a year's wages for the average Jamaican.

Sound system dances were held at outdoor venues called "lawns"—open spaces often adjacent to a bar. Lawns are described by sound system pioneer Winston Blake:

[You] had the most important part of the Jamaican scenario called lawns, like Jubilee Tile Gardens and Chocomo Lawn, big places that were either concrete slab or [surrounded] by wire fence, and you'd have a dance in that area, either at the back of a house or the side of a building—a space where you could put up the [sound system] music. You had control, because there was an entrance gate.[21]

Most of the famous lawns were on Beat Street in Kingston. However, the speakers, amplifiers, and turntables could be set up anywhere there was electricity. Some of this equipment ran on car batteries and could be moved from place to place. Mohair Slim, a deejay on the PBS radio show *Blue Juice*, describes the situation:

> The [sound systems] were sufficiently mobile that an operator could service West Kingston clubgoers at Johnson's Drive-In on Saturday night and be ready for a Sunday afternoon picnic gig at Cane River . . . Some venues had their built-in systems like "Blue Mirror," which was run out of a brothel in Nest Street. Another early "house set" was "Fats Wallo" based in a bordello on the Kingston waterfront. "Fats Wallo" was renowned for its large selection of R&B singles which its sailor clientele unloaded from the port-cities of New Orleans, Tampa and Miami.[22]

There were other economic benefits to the sound system. Operators did not have to pay or accommodate the needs of musicians and bandleaders. As sound system producer Bunny Lee explains:

> Y'see, after the orchestra play [only] an hour, dem stop fi [for] a break, an' dem eat off all the curry goat, an' drink off all the liquor. So the promoter never reep no profit—dem did prove too expensive fi the dance promoter. [The band] alone eat a pot of goat! So when the sound system come now, the sound no tek no break.[23]

Count Machuki: The First Talker

The first dancehall-quality sound system was set up in 1950 by Tom "The Great" Sebastian, the pseudonym of Chinese hardware merchant Thomas Wong. While Sebastian produced the dances, his records were selected by Duke Vin, who got them from a friend who lived in the United States. Vin recalls: "The popular tunes of the time included 'Page Boy Shuffle,' 'Big Jay Shuffle,' 'Coxsone Hop,' [and] 'Downbeat Shuffle.' Those records were tops, and if you didn't have them then people didn't come to your dances. Because people want to hear the sound that was number one at the time."[24]

The popularity of Sebastian's dances spawned several imitators, including Sir Coxsone's Downbeat system, Duke Reid's Trojan system, and Vincent "King" Edwards's Giant system. As competition heated up, record selectors went to great lengths to obtain the hottest selection of songs. Some sent

Coxsone places the needle on a record as a deejay introduces the music. Sound system operators relied on colorful deejays to help keep the crowds dancing.

buyers, called "touts," to hang around wharves so they could purchase records from sailors when ships came in. Others purchased records by mail from the United States. After a few years, sound system operators began traveling to Harlem in New York City, as well as black neighborhoods in Chicago and New Orleans, to search for obscure yet danceable R&B records in stores.

While having the best records was important, sound system operators relied on colorful deejays to keep the crowd dancing at a fever pitch. In 1954, a deejay called Count Machuki changed sound system forever when he began using popular slang to improvise clever spoken introductions, or "toasts," for the records. Machuki, who worked for Sir Coxsone, made his style unique by adding "peps," per-

cussive effects made by clicking the mouth close to the microphone. Machuki, the legendary "first talker," explains how he started on the road to deejay fame:

I said to [Sir Coxsone]: 'Give me the microphone.' He handed me the mike, I started dropping my wisecracks, and [Coxsone] was all for it. . . . I was repeating them all the night through that Saturday. . . . Everybody fell for it. I got more liquor than I could drink that night. . . . Well, I was not satisfied with that. So I said I had to get more things to say. . . . And from there on I was able to create my own jives. The first I wrote for myself was: "If you dig my jive/you're cool and very much alive/Everybody all round town/Machuki's the reason why I shake it down/When it comes to jive/You can't whip him with no stick." That went down with the fans handsomely. And from there on I tried not to repeat myself, started creating. There would be times when the records playing would, in my estimation, sound weak, so I'd put in some peps: chick-a-took, chick-a-took, chick-a-took. That created a sensation![25]

Machuki spawned a host of imitators with names such as Lord Koos of the Universe, King Sporty, and Nation. While blasting out the favorite R&B tunes, or "fave raves," they ordered the dancers to "get some life in your feet, 'cause we're turning up the musical heat!"[26]

Fashion and Dancing

Humorous commentary from deejays was only one attraction to sound system dances. As the center of Jamaican social life, these events inspired people to don their finest fashions and dress to impress their neighbors. Men put on their best suits while women wore petticoats, known as crinolines, under their dresses. During energetic dances like the jitterbug and the bop, the petticoats were shown off as women twirled and were whirled through the air. Bunny Goodison, owner of an early dancehall, recalls the importance of fashion:

Wearing their finest dresses, Jamaican women dance at a large sound system party in this 1950s photo.

I remember in the '50s and '60s people took great pride in how they dressed. Clean, believe you me, clean-clean. That was it because girls don't speak to you unless you look trash [well-dressed], you know what I mean. Cause I remember like [American jazz singer] Billy Eckstine was an icon for we guys, you know. Cause Mr. B was top case. You have some shirts that they call the *rolled collar* that he invented. I mean we were into clothes and, you know two-tone shoes with the likkle [little] holes and ring, you know. People use to clean. . . . People come to be nice. . . . The only thing that was causing a problem those times was if you try to hit 'pon a man's girl or you were having a problem about girl. But nothing else.[27]

The emphasis on fashion was second only to the importance of dancing. Some talented dancers, known as "legs men," were as renowned as sound system deejays. "Pam Pam" Gifford, One-Eye Bostic, Pershom the Cat, and Mister Legs perfected their dances during the big band era and brought them into the sound system venue. During dances, each tried to outdo the other and attract the most attention.

A trick that often captivated the crowd required a full beer bottle and lightning reflexes. In perfect time to the music, a dancer would throw the bottle high in the air, spin in a full circle, and snatch it out of the air before it could smash on the floor. Some dances, how-ever, were so difficult to perform that they actually endangered the physical health of the performers. The dance known as the Yank required people to jerk their hips in a series of drastic movements. While those who could perform the Yank earned the respect of onlookers and their fellow dancers, in-juries were so common that hospitals were full. As Winston Blake recalls: "They had a thing them called the Yank, that was a big dance in Jamaica, so big that a lot of people dislocated their hips doing it. They had a big (an-nouncement) in the paper, 'No bed at hospital for Yankers,' because people Yank themselves out of control."[28]

While not everyone was able to do the Yank, there were few people who did not dance at all. As Blake recalls, if a person could not dance, he or she bet-ter not show up at a sound system lawn:

In our era, you had to be able to dance, if you couldn't dance you got no respect. . . . [Dance] was the god. The sound was important, but what was even more important was the movement to the sound. So if you came to a dance and you couldn't dance, what are you do-ing there! If you couldn't dance, you're a spectator, because there is no way you are going to get a dance with anybody, if you could-n't dance. And if you couldn't dance, you'd be laughed at and jeered. And you realize when you left that thing that there is one emergency that you have in your mind, by the hook or the crook you have to learn to dance. When I use to go to school—college—I made a tidy sum every week out of teaching guys how to dance. So, people were always innovating and imitating. I mean people dance cha-cha, mambo, rock and roll, this, that, [the] jitterbug. I mean we can all do those dances, because it was necessary to do that.[29]

Dance Crashers Mash Up Competition

While dancers rivaled one another for public attention, sound system proprietors were in fierce competition for patrons' money. From the earliest days of sound system, operators scratched the labels off popular R&B records so that competitors could not obtain their own copies of the song. Those who had the best tunes and the loudest sound systems attracted followers who exhibited fanatical devotion to their favorite deejays and selectors. This fierce loyalty has been compared to that exhibited by sports fans, as Barrow and Dalton write: "It was virtually unheard of for someone to enjoy, for instance, Coxsone's Downbeat one week and Duke Reid's Trojan the next: you were either a Coxsone fan or a Reid fan."[30]

Sometimes the competition was formalized in a "battle of the bands" situation. An operator would set up his own lawn adjacent to a competitor and point his piles of speakers directly at another's dance. When the music started, the crowd would decide which deejay and songs they liked better. A single hot record or an original toasting deejay could determine where a crowd spent the night.

By the mid-1950s, competition had grown so fierce that the originator of the style, Tom "The Great" Sebastian, moved from Beat Street to a more peaceful neighborhood closer to Kingston's wealthier residents. Many observers at the time believed that Sebastian was forced to flee by his biggest competitor, Duke Reid, a former police officer who was known for wearing several pistols in his waistband and carrying a rifle wherever he went. Reid dressed in an ermine robe and wore a gold crown. At the beginning of each dance, he was carried to the stage upon the shoulders of his dedicated fans.

Reid's success was built on more than a flamboyant appearance and a powerful sound system. He also employed groups of ex-convicts with names like Dapper Dan, Buggy an' Horse, and Sam Jeggy, who acted as enforcers, or bouncers, at Reid's dances. These men also acted as "dance crashers," who attended dances held by competitors in order to "mash up" or sabotage them. This might be done by starting fights or by cutting cables and damaging speakers and amplifiers.

Reid was not afraid to take matters into his own hands either, as Salewicz explains:

Duke Reid [became] enraged at the ear-splitting volume with which another sound [system] was audaciously playing in his neighbor-

A Jamaican woman swings her jitterbug partner by his legs at a sound system party. Dancers at such parties typically tried to outdo each other.

hood. Going to look for this offender, Reid discovered sounds sailing out of a state-of-the-art jukebox, gaudily replete with all manner of flashing neon lights. Drawing one of the guns he was . . . never without, Duke Reid proceeded to fill the jukebox with a fusillade of [bullets], until it ceased functioning.[31]

Reid's closest competitor was Clement Seymore Dodd, known as Coxsone, whose Downbeat system was one of the most successful in Jamaica. Whereas Reid was in his forties during the sound system heyday, Coxsone was younger and more aware of the latest trends. Coxsone often visited the black communities in Brooklyn, Chicago, and

The Roots of Rhythm and Blues

The roots of rhythm and blues (R&B) music go back at least five centuries to African drum music that highlighted the second and fourth beats, or "backbeats," in each four-beat measure. An emphasis on the backbeat makes people want to clap their hands, tap their feet, and dance. In a very real sense, this stress on the backbeat, called syncopation, is the heartbeat of R&B as well as rock and roll.

Another aspect of tribal music that found its way into rhythm and blues was the traditional singing style known as "call-response," in which a song leader sings a line and a group of singers repeats it. This singing technique was brought to American shores by black slaves who modified it for use in Christian gospel singing. The call-response style was also used in work songs, known as "field hollers." By the end of the nineteenth century, African American musicians were using modified call-response, syncopation, and field hollers in a new style of music called blues. These songs, which incorporated three basic chords, with their flexible gliding melodies, or "blue notes," formed the roots of R&B.

By the 1940s, small combos featuring a guitar, standup bass, piano, drums, and a horn section blended blues with modified big band jazz into a faster R&B style known as "jump blues." This music featured a strong backbeat, hot improvised solos by individual players, and blueslike lyrics shouted over the music. In the 1950s, R&B and jump blues were the favorite musical styles of Jamaicans who attended sound system dances.

elsewhere to find the latest R&B and jazz records. His better taste in music notwithstanding, Coxsone, like Reid, sometimes resorted to violence in order to discourage unfair competitive practices. As he recalls:

When I started, Duke had a bunch of bad guys who come around and try to intimidate you. I remember this instance, I'm there playin' my sound. Machuki's [backing me up], somebody call me because this guy was [lifting] the [playing mechanism] off the record. I came up and show him it was the wrong thing to do. He did this again, and I knocked him out.[32]

Sometimes the competition went beyond the sound system operators as relations between their supporters flared into bloodshed. Brent Dowe was a witness to such violence, as he recalls in *Reggae: The Story of Jamaican Music* by Lloyd Bradley:

> The whole of this area, Bond Street, was Duke Reid followers, they used to say Duke Reid's sound is better than Coxsone's, while Coxsone had his own crowd in his own area. These people used to travel and follow the Duke Reid sound. Anywhere he play, all these people would leave Bond Street and Charles Street just to go where he is at. He had his protection too, "chucker outs", who would damage you if you say anything about Duke Reid or try to damage his sound. They were his men and used to protect him so you couldn't touch his sound. Coxsone had his own protectors too, because each of these sound systems had followers and most of the time they are at war with each other. Real war, fights. Man get chop up, get hurt, just to say Duke Reid's sound is better than Coxsone. A Coxsone man might stab you or a Duke Reid man might stab you if you say the wrong thing. It was a very serious rivalry.[33]

Changing Styles in U.S. Music Prompt Jamaican Innovation

While fans of Coxsone and Reid fought their battles, sound system operators Prince Buster, King Edwards, and dozens of smaller operators provided further rivalry. Ironically, as more operators got into the business, the American records that fueled the sound system style began to grow scarce. With the advent of rock and roll in the mid-1950s, fewer artists were recording the hard-driving rhythm-and-blues sounds loved by Jamaicans. As Chang and Chen write: "Black American records became increasingly slick, self-conscious and soft in the attempt to 'cross over' and appeal to white audiences. The driving beat which moved the sound session dancers was weakening. . . . [Hard] tunes were becoming scarce and business began dropping at the dances."[34]

Stanley Motta, who had set up Jamaica's first recording studio to make mento records, decided to do something to remedy the situation. In 1954 he recorded an R&B record, "Till the End of Time," by the vocal duo Bunny Robinson and Skully Simms. Instead of going to the expense of pressing records of the song, Motta simply put it on a cheap "soft wax," or acetate, record called a "dubplate." Although these records wore out quickly, they were an easy way to get tunes out to sound system operators who played them along with American R&B. Before long, Coxsone, Reid, Edwards, and Prince Buster had all started their own labels to record dubplates for sound systems. Coxsone remembers his first records:

> I searched the U.S. but the R&B supply was drying up. So I decided to record my own music. . . . I had a

couple of sessions, basically tango and calypso and some rhythm and blues inclined sounds. . . . After the first three or four sessions the feedback was really good because the people started dancing. Basically we found a sound that was popular with the dance crowd in Jamaica and worked from there. The songs were really based on dancing.[35]

Producers like Coxsone often had three or four sound systems simultane-ously operating in different areas and were able to record different styles of music that were popular in different regions. This led them to pursue artists who could blend calypso, mento, R&B, and even jazz. As in early island music, the resulting records had a purely Jamaican sound. For example, when Owen Gray made "On the Beach" for Coxsone, he called his band the Coxsonairs and celebrated Sir Coxsone's Downbeat sound system in the lyrics. The concept of a singer praising a

Coxsone, one of the most successful Jamaican sound system operators in the 1950s, and his Downbeat system were a frequent sight at sound system lawns.

The Jamaican Recording Industry

In the 1950s, Jamaican groups often imitated popular American recording artists. In his "The Untold Story of Jamaican Popular Music" Web article, music historian Mohair Slim describes the musicians and their influences:

The output of the Jamaica record industry in 1960 included every species in the Rhythm and Blues genus. From the New York–style Doo Wop [performed by the Jamaican group] The Charmers to Clue J & His Blues Blasters' honkin' instrumentals a la [Philadelphia R&B organist] Bill Doggett. Vocalists Keith & Enid sang syrupy ballads in the style of popular New Orleans duo Gene & Eunice.

The influence on the stars of Jamaican Boogie or "Shuffle" were obvious. Al T. Joe (AKA Jamaica Fats) was a Fats Domino imitator. Wilfred Edwards had the bearing of a Caribbean Nat King Cole. Owen Gray's piano style more than resembled Memphis' Rosco Gordon, a cult hero on the island. . . .

Laurel Aitken was the first Jamaican to reach No. 1 on the local charts—with 1959's 'Boogie In My Bones'/ 'Little Sheila.' Aitken had a particularly authentic Blues sound borrowing from [American blues artists] Amos Milburn and Floyd Dixon in particular. He had a string of hits with 'Boogie Rock', 'Judgment Day' and 'Mary-Lee.' Derrick Morgan, with tracks such as 'Shake A Leg', 'Fat Man' and 'Lover Boy', was one of the biggest stars of the Boogie-Shuffle era. Other hit sounds of the day were 'Easy Snappin' by Theo Beckford (perhaps the first recorded Jamaican blues), 'Please Let Me Go' by Owen Gray, 'Oh Carolina' by the Folkes Brothers and 'Manny-Oh' by Higgs & Wilson.

sound system on record was uniquely Jamaican and continues even today.

The fierce competition among sound system operators was carried over to the recording business. This was clearly demonstrated to singer Derrick Morgan, who recorded the hit song "Lover Boy" for Duke Reid's Treasure Isle label. When Morgan recorded another hit, "Fat Man," for the competing Hi-Lite label, Reid was infuriated. The record producer sent several thugs to pick up

Morgan and bring him to his studio. After warning the singer not to record for anyone else, Reid had Morgan record a song with the remorseful-sounding title "Love Not to Brag."

Jamaican Boogie

The sound system recording business also spawned a popular style known as Jamaican boogie. This sound originated with African American piano players in the 1920s who would play "stride" style, using their left hand to play percussive, "striding" mid-range chords and bass notes while their right hand "tickled" out the melody on the upper keys. By the 1940s, this style was known as boogie woogie and was often accompanied by a stand-up bass playing a fast-paced "walking" bass line. When played by islanders in the 1950s, Jamaican boogie was an up-tempo, hard-driving, blues-based dance music that emphasized the first and third beats of a four-beat measure.

Jamaican boogie records, such as Jivin' Junior's "Lollipop Girl," were so popular that Coxsone played them up to ten times per night. Although crowds loved such songs, the producers did not go to the trouble of pressing them into records. In 1958, however, someone asked Coxsone if he could sell records of his acetates. Coxsone scoffed, be-

lieving that Jamaicans were not interested in listening to Saturday-night dance music at home. However, he allowed the man to run off a few hundred 45 rpm records, which sold out immediately. Within days, Coxsone and the others were pressing singles for sale at dances and in stores.

While most songs were not major hits, a few might sell twenty or thirty thousand copies. As was typical in the music business everywhere at the time, the creative talent who wrote, sang, and played on the records did not make much money. They were typically paid less then $20 per song, and some wrote and recorded a new song each week in order to earn a living. Since the recording artists barely got paid, King Edwards recalls: "At that time it was what we call free music."[36] However, an artist who cut a popular record would be able to book live engagements where the pay was better.

By the 1960s, sound systems blasting Jamaican music were part of island life and formed a basis for the music styles that were to follow, such as ska and reggae. As Katz writes in *Solid Foundation*: "The advent of the sound system was extremely important to Jamaica's popular culture, particularly as it was a defining element in setting up the island's home-grown music industry."[37]

Chapter Three

Ska and Rocksteady

Politics have long played a role in the evolution of indigenous Jamaican music. Almost from Jamaica's earliest times as a colony, Jonkanoo was a way for slaves to exhibit a rebellious streak, while in the early twentieth century mento sometimes provided a format for humorous commentary on political events. On August 6, 1962, a new era of Jamaican political history was initiated when the country gained independence from Great Britain after three hundred years of colonial rule. While 70 percent of the nation's people continued to live below the official poverty line, independence served to brighten the mood for many. As Bradley writes in *Reggae: The Story of Jamaican Music*: "With independence looming, the notion of being Jamaican took on a very different meaning, and one of the most obvious, instantly uplifting ways of expressing this notion of nationalism was with a modern Jamaican music form."[38]

This form, called ska, was a composite of R&B, fast blues, and boogie but with a different beat. While boogie has a driving 4/4 rhythm, where every beat is emphasized, ska guitar players highlighted single strums, or "chops," on the offbeat. The concept of emphasizing the offbeat is described by Mohair Slim: "If you imagine a drummer hitting down on each of the four beats, the strum was made at the point at which the drummer would raise his stick rather than when he hit—'a-ska, a-ska, a-ska, a-ska.' The bouncy tempo thus produced could be augmented by employing a horn section or a harmonica (single-note riffing) in support of the guitar."[39] This danceable, syncopated music was played at a rapid, galloping tempo, with drum rolls pushing the rhythm, and horn players blowing melodic jazz riffs (improvised phrases).

Ska singers often added soulful three- or four-part harmonies, but these also differed from Jamaican boogie. In boogie, vocalists imitated American R&B singers, whereas ska singers used Jamaican patois, purposely slurring their

A deejay spouts nonsense lyrics as he makes a toast.

words. They also utilized African melodic concepts—often heard in Pocomania churches—where singers chanted unintelligible words, noises, and sounds in a complex rhythmic pattern known as polyrhythm. This improvised string of nonsensical syllables with vocal growls and rumbles was known as "scat singing," a technique popularized in the late 1920s by American jazz player Louis Armstrong. Nonsense lyrics were also used by

deejays such as Machuki when toasting at sound system lawns.

"Hail Skavoovie!"

While ska vocals may have had traditional roots, the term itself was as new as the musical style. Tommy McCook, saxophonist for the pioneering ska group the Skatalites, says the word *ska* came from the word *Skavoovie*. This term was often used as a salutation by Cluette "Clue J" Johnson, who played bass with the boogie band the Blues Blasters. As McCook stated in an interview: "Skavoovie is a greeting. That's the way [Clue J] used to greet you, even long before ska came in. Instead of saying 'What's up, Jack?' or 'Hello, Ronnie' . . . he would say, 'What happen, Skavoovie?' or 'Hail Skavoovie!'"[40]

McCook not only knows how the term *ska* was coined, he was in the studio the day the first ska grooves were laid down on record. As he recalls, Coxsone Dodd was the man responsible: "It was conscious, consciously done. . . . Dodd asked someone in the studio what could he do to change the effect of the blues concept . . . someone, whoever it was, introduced that up-beat which is referred to as the so-called 'Ska.'"[41] Coxsone immediately realized that the sound was not only truly original but also had great commercial potential.

The musicians who were present in the studio that day were part of Jamaica's tight-knit musical community. The new beat caught on quickly and spread like wildfire as the musicians showed it to others. Before long, each studio had its own session bands composed of the island's finest musicians, those who were accustomed to playing a wide variety of music including mento, R&B, jazz, and ska. These players followed musical scores written by arrangers who composed catchy sounds that were used to back whatever vocalist happened to be singing the song. This system created a paradoxical situation where the quality of the music played by the backing band was often better than the vocals or even the song itself. However, most ska songs only had a few verses, leaving plenty of space for hot instrumental breaks from studio musicians such as McCook, Roland Alphonso on saxophone, and Don Drummond on trombone.

These musicians, and others, provided a cohesive, high-quality sound from studio to studio because most had a common musical background. Nearly all studio players on the island had attended the

The Ska Beat

Before the ska style was invented, most popular music in Jamaica, and elsewhere, had a familiar beat. The second and fourth beats of each four-beat measure were emphasized by the rhythm instruments. However, as Kevin O'Brien Chang and Wayne Chen write in Reggae Routes, *"the ska rhythm was something completely different":*

[Ska] is a fusion of Jamaican mento rhythm with R&B, with the drum coming on the 2nd and 4th beats and the guitar emphasizing the up [strumming up from the highest to the lowest strings on] the 2nd, 3rd, and 4th beats. The drum therefore is carrying the blues and swing beats of the American music and the guitar expressing the mento sound. . . . [The] afterbeat, strummed by a rhythm guitar or played on the piano, came to be characteristic of the form. No one instrument really predominates— horns and saxes emphasize the guitar chordal beat, the bass often strides in American walking bass fashion and the drum provides the basic 4/4 framework.

Trumpeter Johnny "Dizzy" Moore has a very interesting insight into the source of the "ska" beat. He considered the European "martial" drumming he encountered at Alpha Boys School and in the army as the strongest influence on his playing and one of the key influences on the development of ska.

Alpha Boys School, an institution for wayward boys founded by Roman Catholic nuns in the 1880s. By 1890, the school had a drum and fife corps, which was later transformed into a brass band. In the 1930s and 1940s, the Alpha School band served as a training ground for McCook and Drummond, along with other top ska players, such as trumpeters Johnny "Dizzy" Moore and Eddie Thornton, trombonist Rico Rodriguez, and dozens of others.

With most ska players sharing similar musical roots, it was inevitable that the infectious music they produced would include snatches of other styles. This likely contributed to the success of the music among the dancehall crowds, as Bradley writes:

> Since ska wasn't too radical a departure from its American counterpart it was easy for the sound system crowds to love it. It was up-tempo and joyously celebratory; could incorporate such local flavour as [traditional] drumming or snatches of mento . . . ; its export was putting Jamaica on the world culture map; and as a music to dance to, it was close enough to R&B to be familiar. But ska came to dominate Jamaican culture, and this was [because of] the musicians involved and how they took to it.[42]

The Sounds of Independence

The popularity of the new musical form was undoubtedly boosted by the co-incidence of its appearance on the music scene at a time when Jamaicans were filled with national pride over the nation's recent independence. Ska soon came to be seen as a truly original product of an otherwise poor nation. The early lyrics to some ska songs used independence as a theme. As Derrick Morgan sings in "Forward March":

> Gather together brothers and sisters for independence
>
> We're Independent!
>
> Join hands to hands children, start to dance we're independent
>
> We're Independent!
>
> Don't be sullen, no, the lord is still with you
>
> Because the time has come, when you can have your fun, so tag along.[43]

Other lyrics appealed to ska's core fans in the shantytowns of West Kingston. As Chris Wilson writes in the CD liner notes to *Original Club Ska*, "The inside jokes, the rivalries, the common symbolism, and the shared experiences of ghetto life were the fabric of this musical tapestry."[44]

Ska might have remained in the Kingston slums were it not for a prominent white politician in Jamaican government. Edward Seaga, who would become prime minister in 1980, was a Harvard-educated anthropologist. Seaga began producing records in the late 1950s and was named Jamaica's minister of culture and development in 1962. He believed that the country needed its own popular music as an independent nation. He asked mento recording artist Carlos Malcolm to help popularize ska.

Malcolm noticed that much of the ska that was popular in the city was rough, with musicians playing the wrong chords on out-of-tune guitars. In August 1962, Malcolm recruited some of the island's most talented musicians, including Jimmy Cliff, the Blues Busters, and Toots Hibbert and the Maytals to play a concert called "Ska Goes Uptown" at a club in a middle-class neighborhood. As Malcolm tells it:

> Some high toned people criticized us for bringing such low class music uptown, but it was a big success. Radio picked up on the sound and middle-class Jamaicans started buying ska records. I would never try to take credit for being one of ska's creators. But we helped to shape it as a music and we were . . . primarily responsible for spreading it around Kingston and around Jamaica on live shows.[45]

In the years that followed, ska followed divergent paths. Some bands, particularly Byron Lee & the Dragonaires, played "uptown ska," a softer, mellower version of the style. The rhythms were less complex, and the lyrics did

Early ska star Toots Hibbert performs with his group the Maytals. Hibbert was one of several performers who helped to popularize ska music across Jamaica.

not emphasize politics, black pride, or social protest. Those from the ghetto played "downtown ska"—loud, fast, sexy, and filled out with hot, improvised riffs and sometimes controversial lyrics.

Whether or not a band played downtown ska, the music certainly caught the attention of Kingston's wealthier "uptown" residents. These people, however, were more interested in making money than dancing to the latest sounds. With Coxsone and other producers piling up huge sums, many nonmusical people tried to get into the ska game. As Goodison recalls, however, an element of national pride also came into play:

> You find people who normally wouldn't be near it, [becoming] producers now, executive producers, [who] put the money up, get the artist and get records being cut, because it became a profitable venture. . . . And I would imagine by independent '62 where the strong surge . . . of national pride . . . must have sort of had impact . . . because all the symbols now which represented Jamaica were being embraced . . . and none more so [than the music].[46]

The Skatalites Arrive on the Scene

The popularity of ska changed the Jamaican music scene by once again making live music popular. By 1964, sound systems were in direct competition with ska bands for the attention of Jamaica's youth. Live music venues also served as meeting places for Jamaica's best musicians. They brought together a group of former jazz players who became closely associated with the ska sound.

The Skatalites played their first gig on June 27, 1964, at the Hi Hat Club in Kingston but had been jamming together regularly since the late 1940s. Like most classic ska bands, the group was large. Its nine founding members included three saxophone players, a trumpet player, a trombonist, a pianist, a drummer, a bass guitarist, and guitarist.

Some of the group's members were present at ska's inception when Coxsone put together the new sound, and Coxsone remained central to the Skatalites' promotion. He supplied the sound system, microphones, guitar amplifiers, and other equipment while providing transportation, promotion, and bookings. He also recorded the band in studio. Ironically, McCook, who was among the originators of the sound, was a reluctant member of the Skatalites. As a dedicated jazzman, the tenor-sax player was wary of the sound, and initially opposed being in the band. After their initial performance at the Hi Hat Club, however, the band was in demand all over the island, and it was hard for McCook to argue with success.

For some performances the Skatalites added four vocalists who were entertainers as well as singers. One vocalist, Jackie Opel, was said to sing like popular American soul vocalist Jackie Wilson

One of the most popular ska bands, the Skatalites performed to huge crowds of frenzied dancers in venues throughout the island.

and dance like R&B superstar James Brown. Possessing an incredible six-octave range, Opel could "drop legs," that is, do the splits while belting out a tune. In the liner notes for *Ska Foundation: The Skatalites*, Brian Keyo describes the activities at Skatalites shows:

> The Skatalites proved a solid draw; the nine musicians had their followings, the band featured guest soloists and singers, and audience participation was encouraged by "launching" the band [like a rocket] to start each show. [Singer] Lord Tanamo started the countdown, and then Jackie Opel made it tradition. At certain venues such as the Odeon, during the show a satellite moving through space was projected onto the wall behind the band! Antics included

Johnny Moore twirling his trumpet and [Lloyd] Brevett swinging his bass during breaks in tunes. Dancers such as Jabba, Pam Pam, Persian, and a rumba queen named Madame Pussycat, gained fame by dropping legs during Skatalites shows.[47]

The Skatalites Break Up but Leave a Legacy

The Skatalites' reign as the kings of the ska scene was brief. As with many supergroups composed of talented musicians who are already stars in their own right, there were personality clashes from the start. Problems were magnified by other troubles as well. Many say the band was never the same after trombonist Drummond, who suffered from mental illness, stabbed his girlfriend to death on New Year's Day 1965 and had to be

A Jamaican man demonstrates some fast and furious dance moves at a Skatalite concert. Many Skatalite fans sustained injuries while dancing at the band's shows.

institutionalized. A few months after the band's first-anniversary gig, the Skatalites disbanded.

Although their time at the top was short, the Skatalites' creativity broke new ground. They applied the bouncy tempo and galloping pace of ska to many popular songs. This gave the band great range and allowed them to play ska versions of hits, including the Beatles' "I Shoulda Known Better," the theme song from the movie *Exodus*, and Duke Ellington's jazz great "Caravan," which was renamed "Skaravan."

When the Skatalites were in their prime, dancing at their concerts was so

frenzied that many fans sustained injuries. Indeed, at a show at the Club Calypso in Falmouth, a nurse who worked at a nearby hospital allegedly danced herself to death. Typically, however, ska dancing was less dangerous, as Reckord explains:

[Ska] came with its own set of movements—a kind of charade to music, in which the dancers brought into play domestic activity (washing clothes, bathing), recreation (horseracing, cricket), anything that appealed to the ska dancer in the moment. Some real fast and furious "footworks" came out of the ska period.[48]

Ska International

Ska was the first Jamaican musical style that was exported to other nations. At the height of its popularity in 1964, ska music was briefly heard in the soundtrack of the James Bond movie *Dr. No*, filmed in Jamaica. More important, Seaga sent several ska artists, including Jimmy Cliff, the Blues Busters, and Byron Lee & the Dragonaires, to the world's fair held in New York City in 1964. Among the artists was Millie Small, who scored an international hit with the ska song "My Boy Lollipop," recorded in the United Kingdom. The world's fair engagement led to regular appearances at New York's prestigious Copacabana. Recording giant Atlantic, hoping to cash in on the new American ska craze, hired Lee to record an album called *The Real Jamaica Ska*. The craze soon peaked, however, and the album did not sell well. Mohair Slim comments about the reception of ska by the American public: "While the Ska fad lasted only about six months and the immediate benefit of the hype was received by only a select few, it is significant that, for the first time, the US public had been given a taste of the rich musical culture of an island only a few hundred miles south of the Florida Peninsula."[49]

The ska style had more success in the United Kingdom, where British consumers were more often exposed to the cultures of the East and West Indian regions that were part of Great Britain's colonial empire for hundreds of years. In addition, many Jamaicans lived in London and were aware of musical trends emanating from their homeland.

Several record labels were established to cater to the British ska market, including Blue Beat, Doctor Bird, and R&B/Skabeat. Most simply rereleased ska songs that had been hits in Jamaica, but driven by the international success of "My Boy Lollipop," large English record companies such as EMI, London, and Parlophone began to record British-based ska artists. This music was enjoyed by Jamaican immigrants, but when it became trendy among English white youth, its success was guaranteed.

Although the state-owned radio channel BBC (British Broadcasting Company) refused to play ska, some of the songs recorded in that style outsold the "Top 40" ones that were played on the radio. For example, within five days of its release, nineteen thousand ska fans snapped up "Housewives' Choice," a record by Derrick & Patsy. By 1970, ska was too huge for the BBC to disregard, and the station finally started playing songs in that style. Almost immediately, Prince Buster's "Al Capone" became the first ska hit to make it into the Top 40.

Ska's impact in Britain was long lasting. Although it disappeared for a time, the style was revived in the late 1970s and early 1980s by the English bands The Specials, Madness, and The Beat. In the 1990s it was once again revived on the other side of the Atlantic, in a different form, by American group No Doubt.

Ska in England

Many Jamaicans migrated to England in the second half of the twentieth century. Far from the tropical warmth of their native land, Jamaicans did what they could to bring a little musical sunshine to their daily lives. Mohair Slim explains in his "The Untold Story of Jamaican Popular Music" Web article:

In the cold and unfamiliar environment of post-War industrial England, expatriate Jamaicans sought succor by reviving aspects of their lives in Jamaica. On any given weekend in London, numerous "Blues parties" took place at which the black community—manual labourers, merchant seaman and students alike—gathered to dance, drink, smoke and catch up with news from back home. Sound systems emulating those of Kingston sprung up to pack out the Town Halls and Community Centres. . . .

The high cost and difficulty of obtaining new release Jamaican Shuffle/Ska [45 rpm records] was a significant problem for the British enthusiast. As there was no distribution network for Jamaican records in England, they had to be specially imported from the Caribbean. Jewish entrepreneur [Emil] Shallit was the owner of the London-based Melodisc Records. Since its founding in 1946, Melodisc had been releasing Jazz, Calypso and other exotic sounds Shallit discovered on his travels. In 1960, Shallit launched a new label aimed specifically at London's West Indian market. As a vehicle for local release of Jamaican musical product, it was so successful that, in England, the label's name, "Blue Beat," became synonymous with "Ska."

The inaugural release on Blue Beat Records was 1960's "Boogie Rock" by Laurel Aitken who had immigrated to Britain earlier in the year. Aitken, already an established star in Jamaica, was to become the patriarch of England's Ska and Reggae movements.

Rocking to Rocksteady

Ironically, as ska's popularity was ascending in England in the mid-1960s, the music was quickly losing popularity in the land of its birth. By 1967, only five years after its inception, ska was dead in Jamaica. It had been replaced by a slower, mellower sound called rocksteady, or rock steady. Comparing the two, Katz writes: "If ska hit the newly independent Jamaica with the force of Hurricane Hattie, then rock steady arrived in the shape of a cool breeze nestled in the calm after the storm."[50]

Ska and rocksteady differed musically in several respects. Whereas the horns dominated the sound in ska, they were used as complementary background instruments in rocksteady. The rocksteady beat was slower and the rhythm was emphasized differently. Instead of the guitarist hitting the offbeat, the rocksteady rhythm was known as the "one drop" because the drummer hit the deep-toned bass drum or floor tom once, on the third beat of every measure. This made for music of a mellower pace, allowing dancers to "rock steady" in one place.

Bob Marley performs in a Kingston club in 1969. As ska music waned in popularity, it was replaced by the slower, softer rocksteady style of Marley and others.

The most important change in rocksteady concerned the bass line. In the ska style, the bass was relegated to the background and generally drowned out by the loud, blaring horns. In rocksteady the bass was prominently featured. As Coxsone states, in rocksteady, "the bass would be playing a steady sort of melody in the background. We tried to make it rock steady with a real catchy beat and steady for dancing. Rocksteady was when we realized how important a steady catchy bass line was."[51]

Rude Boys

During the height of the rocksteady era, some of Jamaica's youth listened to an entirely different style of music. Known as rudeboy music, the style is defined by its driving, electric bass line and its lyrics about gangsters and ghetto life. The rude-boy phenomenon is explained by Stephen Davis in Reggae Bloodlines:

In Jamaica in the late Sixties most of the younger, up-and-coming . . . performers sprang out of the "Rude Boy" phenomenon. Rudies were young men, aged anywhere between fourteen and thirty (most Jamaican youths leave school at fourteen if not earlier), who had joined the migration from country to Kingston. With no skills and Jamaica's chronic 35-per-cent unemployment rate, the Rudies redefined street life (hanging out, flicking deadly German ratchet knives, trolleyhopping, purse-snatching, occasional muggings, petty theft, rum, insolence, ganja [marijuana], singing, and general hooliganism) into lifetime careers, most of which ended very early. For the Rudie the only way out of the gross tropical shantytowns of West Kingston . . . was via a hit single or a police bullet. The ethos of Rude Boy was pure punk—being the most relentless, outrageous, rudest, best-looking, baddest character [in town]. And the archetypal Rude Boy was [sung about in] the Slickers' "Johnnie Too Bad":

Walking down the road with a pistol in your waist

Johnny you're too bad

Walking down the road with a ratchet in your waist?

Johnny you're too bad

You're jesta robbing and stabbing and looting and shooting

Y'know you're too bad. . . .

This Jamaican youth is a Rude Boy, a member of a 1960s subculture centered around violence and destructive behavior

The vocals were another important aspect of rocksteady; as Bradley writes, it was a "period when singing ruled the grooves and consummated the people's relationship with song."[52] The increased importance of singers had as much to do with the economics of the music business as it did with the new style of music. By the mid-1960s, singers were lining up every morning outside studios hoping to get auditions from record producers. Unlike the schooled jazz musicians who played ska, these young, eager vocalists were much easier for producers to exploit. And while it made financial sense to hire these inexperienced singers, they also had new ideas for music. Up-and-coming musicians were tired of the ska beat in any case, as Bob Marley explains: "[We] don't want to stand around playing and singing the ska beat anymore. The young musicians, dem have a different beat. It was rocksteady now, eager to go!"[53]

The younger players also added more of a political viewpoint to their lyrics. By this time, the initial glow of Jamaican independence had faded and most realized that little had changed since the colonial days. High unemployment, poverty, and a repressive police force provided inspiration for rocksteady lyrics. In 1968, the lyrics to the Ethiopians' hit "Everything Crash" made a reference to the dozens of labor strikes that were taking place throughout the country. The lyrics were perceived as revolutionary by radio programmers, and it was the first song without sexually charged lyrics to be banned in Jamaica. Another song, the Maytals' "54-46 Is My Number" is named after the number the band's founder, Toots Hibbert, was assigned when he was arrested on false charges of marijuana possession in 1967. The lyrics, a contemptuous commentary on the Jamaican justice system, propelled the song to instant number-one status.

With lyrics both scathing and sweet, the rocksteady era is considered by many to be one of the most creative periods in Jamaican musical history. As Chang and Chen write: "Never before or since. . . . was music at the same time so melodically sweet, rhythmically engrossing and lyrically interesting."[54]

Changing Music Forever

The style also changed Jamaican music forever, as Barrow and Dalton write: "The brief flowering of rock steady—between the autumn of 1966 and the summer of 1968—was the most important episode in Jamaica in musical history, exerting an influence on almost every subsequent development. The shift of rhythmic focus onto the bass and drums has remained a feature of all later stages of Jamaican music."[55]

Rocksteady's reign was as short as it was sweet. In 1968 the Maytals released the song "Do the Reggay," and it was the first time the word *reggae* was used in a song. Performed with a combination of rocksteady and ska, it spawned Jamaica's most enduring musical tradition of all. With its roots in Africa, mento, and the Pocomania church, reggae would change the musical tastes of not only Jamaica, but the entire world.

Chapter Four

Bob Marley and the Reggae Explosion

The reggae music played by artists such as Bob Marley and the Wailers, Burning Spear, and Black Uhuru has influenced popular music throughout the world. While it is now heard on every continent, reggae has a pure Jamaican heritage, and the genre has much in common with the styles that preceded it. Like ska and rocksteady, reggae was born in the ghettos of West Kingston. Its rhythms have African roots that can be traced back to the burru music of earlier centuries. And reggae lyrics often express the viewpoint common to those who have fought repression and the colonial system for centuries.

The question of who made the first reggae record is a matter of dispute. The Maytals' single "Do the Reggay" is itself closer to the rocksteady style. There are differences, however. The bass line in the song drives the beat a little bit harder than rocksteady while the guitar, in typical reggae fashion, strums a sharp chord to accent the sec-

ond and fourth beats of each measure. While not pure roots reggae, the song may be considered a transitional link between rocksteady and reggae.

As far as the creator of the first "true" reggae song, musicians disagree. Some say Larry and Alvin's "Nanny Goat" was the first, while Alva Lewis says it was his guitar sound on the song "Bangarang" that made that song the first reggae record. Meanwhile, Gladdy Anderson claims to have invented the sound with his bubbling, fast-paced organ shuffle on "Everybody Bawling." Producer Bunny Lee agrees with Anderson, saying, "That was how reggae developed. From that organ shuffle with the rest of the music falling into place around that."[56]

The origins of the word *reggae* are also unclear. Some say it originated as the word *streggae*, a slang term for prostitute. Others say it defines the "ragged" rhythm of "Do the Reggay." Maytals leader Toots Hibbert states that the word simply came up in conversation, and that its meaning changed over time:

[I was] talking nonsense one day and I just said, "Come on man, let's do the reggae." And later we decide to make a song out of that. It was just a word you would hear on the streets. I don't remember why I apply it to music. . . . At first reggae sort of mean untidy or scruffy. But then it start to mean like coming from the people. Everyday things. From the ghetto to the majority. Things people use like food, we just put music to. Reggae mean regular people who are suffering, and don't have what they want.[57]

"A Voice from the Ghetto"

Whoever coined the term or invented the sound, by the end of 1968, reggae singles were flying out of Jamaica's recording studios with the same frequency as rocksteady and ska in a previous era. Like those earlier styles, reggae lyrics spoke to shantytown residents about the life they knew in Kingston. These were described by poet Sam Brown as:

In this 1969 photo, Bob Marley, Peter Tosh, and Bunny Wailer (left to right) pose in front of their Kingston recording studio.

Reggae's African Roots

In Bass Culture, *Lloyd Bradley states that Lee "Scratch" Perry's "People Funny Boy" was among the first reggae records. However, in typical Jamaican fashion, the song combined musical styles that had been heard on the island for centuries:*

Listen to Lee Perry's 1968 single "People Funny Boy" and, essentially you're listening to Africa. As it was in the sixteenth century. . . . However, concentrate a bit harder and you will notice "People Funny Boy" has a subtly changed structure that differentiates it completely from the rocksteady of the preceding couple of years. True, it might still emphasize the off-beat, but there's much more going on than that slightly higher tempo; crucially, the electric bass is much more up-front and almost metronomically metered, while several guitars are used rhythmically rather than merely melodically. It's those guitars that produce a speedy strumming pattern not unlike mento's banjoes, while the overall measured percussiveness leaves all sorts of holes that are artfully filled in with [the African drums] Burru- and Kumina [Pukanina]-style rhythmic statements. So, a little way beneath the surface lies a Jamaicanness so intrinsic that it doesn't need to worry about the here and the now as it draws a line—a thick black line—straight back to Africa. . . . Although perhaps not a textbook example of reggae, [the] 1968 release date makes ["People Funny Boy"] one of the earliest records to sound the part.

Tin can houses, old and young, [mangy] dogs, rats, inhuman stench Unthinkable conditions that cause the stoutest heart to wrench. . . . Emaciated people, many giving up the ghost, their spirits broken, their gloom deepens.[58]

Bob Marley, born in early 1945 in a small rural village called Nine Mile, was one of the young men who grew up listening to ska, rocksteady, and reggae as he struggled to survive in Kingston's Trench Town slum. His father, Captain Norval Marley, was a wealthy white military officer who was the superintendent of lands for the British government. His mother, Cedella, was a black woman descended from slaves, whose husband abandoned her at age seventeen when she became pregnant with Bob. In 1950 Cedella moved to Kingston, hoping to secure a brighter future for her son, then five years old.

Marley grew up with two friends, Neville Livingston (later known as Bunny Wailer) and Peter Macintosh (who shortened his last name to Tosh). In the early 1960s, Marley, Wailer, and Tosh formed a vocal group. When he was eighteen years old, Marley began writing songs, and the lyrics contained biting social commentary. In 2005, years after the artist's death, *Rolling Stone* writer Mikal Gilmore took a look back: "Marley found qualities of ruthless honesty, courage and rough beauty in tenement-yard community, and he didn't necessarily want to transcend or escape it—instead, to describe its reality and speak for its populace, which was subject to not only destitution but easy condemnation as well."[59]

One of Marley's earliest songs, "Simmer Down," addressed the gang violence of Trench Town, warning gang members that they should control their tempers so as to avoid getting "dropped," or killed, by police. Marley took his song to Coxsone Dodd, by then Jamaica's leading producer, who recorded a ska version the next day with Jamaica's finest studio musicians, the Skatalites. When "Simmer Down" debuted on Coxsone's sound system the following night, it became an instant hit "and for a good reason," as Gilmore writes:

For the first time, a voice from the ghetto was speaking to others who lived in the same straits, acknowledging their existence and giving voice to their troubles, and that breakthrough had a transformative effect, on both the scene and on Marley and his group. . . . Marley had already found one of the major themes that would characterize his songwriting through his entire career.[60]

Ras Tafari: The Black Messiah

Marley began working for Coxsone, living in a back room in his studio and helping other vocal groups rehearse their harmonies. One of those artists, Rita Anderson, was a talented singer who led a band called the I-Threes.

Anderson married Marley in 1966, the same year Ethiopian emperor Haile Selassie visited Jamaica. At Kingston's Norman Manley International Airport, Selassie was greeted by the largest crowd ever gathered there, more than one hundred thousand cheering people. On the tarmac, some waved palm leaves; some the red, green, and gold Ethiopian flag adorned with the insignia of a roaring lion. Others blew the Maroon abeng in welcome. Selassie's appearance was of deep significance to members of a Jamaican religious cult called Rastafarians, or Rastafari.

The Rastafarian religion developed around 1930 when Selassie, whose real name was Ras Tafari, was crowned king of Ethiopia. Rastafarians believed that the African monarch was a Living God, and veneration of Selassie remains central to Rastafarian belief today. Rastas formally call the emperor

A Rastafarian waves a palm frond to welcome Emperor Haile Selassie to Jamaica in 1966. Rastafarians believe that Selassie was the black messiah.

the King of Kings, Elect of God, Conquering Lion of Judah, and the supreme god, Jah. They believe he is the returned messiah, a black Jesus unlike the "white" Jesus commonly portrayed in Christian art. Rastafarians believe that Ethiopia is the true paradise, or Zion, and that Jah has returned to bring relief to the world's long-repressed black people by leading them back to Africa. Among the more controversial Rasta-

farian views is that marijuana, called "ganja," is a holy herb. It is smoked in large quantifies ostensibly to bring Rastas closer to a deeper understanding of their religion and themselves.

Rita Marley was among the thousands who lined the streets on Saturday, April 23, as Selassie's car followed a parade route to a civic reception in downtown Kingston. When the waving Selassie passed Marley, she believes,

The Rastafarian Culture

The lyrics to reggae songs are heavily influenced by the Rastafarian religion, native to Jamaica. A detailed explanation of Rastafarian culture was included on the DVD edition of the 1978 Jamaican reggae film Rockers *directed by Ted Bafaloukos:*

The most important force behind black Jamaican counterculture, and Reggae music, is the Rastafarian faith. In 1930, an Ethiopian prince named Ras Tafari Makkonen was crowned Emperor Haile Selassie I; several Jamaican preachers maintained that the Emperor was the messiah. The most important of these early preachers, L.P. Howell, formulated the principles of the Rastafarian movement. . . . To escape persecution [for their religious beliefs], Howell and his followers established communes in remote rural areas, where they developed such customs as the use of ganja (marijuana) as an aid to religious meditation, and the wearing of their hair in the natural lion-like "Dreadlock" style.

In 1954, the police [raided and destroyed] Howell's rural settlements. But, rather than destroying the movement this event set the stage for its growth. Rastafarianism largely relocated to Kingston slums and became a pervasive, unofficial mass movement which dominated the cultural life of Jamaica's oppressed majority. . . .

To preserve his independence from [decadent Western society, called] "Babylon," the Rasta man does not beg or work for wages. He prefers to earn his livelihood by self-employment skills such as farming or fishing, by participating in communal workshops, by developing a craft that insures his economic independence.

The lyrics of reggae songs are heavily inspired by the beliefs of Rastafarians like this man.

she saw stigmata, or bloody marks resembling the crucifixion wounds of Jesus, on his hands. Convinced that Selassie was indeed the black Jesus, Rita grew dreadlocks and thereafter devoted her life to Rastafarianism.

In the coming years, Bob Marley would also become a Rastafarian, and his deeply held beliefs would influence every aspect of his music. Marley's lyrics in songs such as "Positive Vibrations," "One Love," "Concrete Jungle," "Revolution," and "War" were informed by the Rastafarian concerns for social justice and the attribution of many wrongs to Babylon, the political and economic systems of Western society.

The Harder They Come

Throughout the late 1960s and early 1970s, as Marley became ever more devoted to Rastafarianism, he recorded with the Wailers but remained solely a Jamaican phenomenon, largely unheard anywhere else. The world was mostly unaware of Rastafarians, reggae, and Jamaican life in general until the 1972 movie *The Harder They Come* was released in theaters in the United States and Great Britain.

The Harder They Come tells the tale of Ivan O. Martin, a fictional character based on a real Jamaican folk hero of the 1940s, a man known as Rhygin. Singer/songwriter Jimmy Cliff played Martin, a country boy who arrived in Kingston with no money and few prospects. However, he was talented enough to get his song "The Harder They Come" made into a record. Al-

This still shot from the 1972 movie The Harder They Come *shows Jimmy Cliff as the outlaw Ivan O. Martin.*

though the catchy song was hit material, the producer offered Martin only $20 for it. Martin himself tried to market the single to sound system operators and deejays but found that they could not play anything not given to them by the producer. Labeled a troublemaker, Martin turned to selling ganja to make a living. In Jamaica at this time, the illegal trade was controlled by police, and in the film Martin kills several police officers in a shootout. Instead of disappearing, he becomes like Rhygin, a well-known outlaw, distributing photos of himself dressed as a rude boy—that is, a rebel—and wielding several pistols. Such provocative acts soon net Martin the status of Jamaica's most wanted criminal, and he is killed by the police. The song, which has become extremely popular, lives on.

The movie's soundtrack features some of Jamaica's hottest tracks, with Cliff singing "You Can Get It If You Really Want," "Sitting in Limbo," "Many Rivers to Cross," and the title song. In addition, a studio scene shows Toots and the Maytals singing "Sweet and Dandy," while other songs such as "Rivers of Babylon" by the Melodians play during dramatic scenes. Until the posthumous release of Bob Marley's *Legend* album in 1984, the soundtrack for *The Harder They Come* was the best-selling reggae album in history.

The movie, written and directed by Perry Henzell, showed the reality of the Jamaican record business as well as the island's social ills. As Bradley writes in *Bass Culture*:

> [*The Harder They Come*] remains the most frank, entertaining and poignant take on any record business, anywhere in the world. . . . [It] opened the curtains on a window that offered an unobstructed panorama across the Kingston studios, producers, artists and the business's internal politics of ex-

ploitation. . . . It offered a razor-sharp insight into what ghetto living was *really* all about. . . . The movie was acted, scripted and directed with such smoldering intensity you could smell the rubbish in the street and feel the heat of the sun. Which was exactly how the music should be approached, as part of a whole—as part of black life in Jamaica—rather than as a separate entity.[61]

The Harder They Come quickly became a cult hit, especially in the United States and Great Britain, and played at midnight movie showings for years after its release. Many credit the movie with popularizing Rastafarian culture and reggae music across the globe, giving instant legitimacy to Jamaican music both at home and abroad. The film also demonstrated that reggae was more than happy music with a great beat. The music, in turn, represented the social, political, religious, and economic elements of Jamaican society.

Catch a Fire
One of the financial backers of *The Harder They Come* was record producer Chris Blackwell, the son of an Englishman and a Jamaican Jewish heiress whose family made a fortune in the rum, sugar, coconut, and cattle trades. Blackwell was uninterested in the family enterprises, however, and founded Island Records in 1960. While recording local artists, Blackwell discovered that there was a better market

for his records in England, so he moved his offices there in 1962. In 1964 Blackwell produced "My Boy Lollipop," and when the single sold more than 7 million copies worldwide, Island's success was assured. By the early 1970s, Island was producing records by some of the biggest stars of the day, including Traffic, Jethro Tull, Cat Stevens, and Robert Palmer. Blackwell never forgot his island roots, however, and promoted various Jamaican artists over the years, distributing records by the Wailers and others in Great Britain.

In the late 1960s, around the time *The Harder They Come* was being filmed, Bob Marley approached Blackwell and asked him whether he would produce a Wailers album. Although several Jamaican producers had found the band members difficult to work with, Blackwell lent the Wailers a small amount of money to produce a record. The group recorded its first album, *Catch a Fire*, in Jamaica and sent the tapes to Blackwell in England.

Blackwell was very pleased with what he heard. The record, unlike previous reggae albums, was not just a collection of singles but was rather a seamless, cohesive unit, each song meshing well with the next. Despite the mastery of the Wailers, Blackwell believed that with further production, the album could be successfully marketed to white rock audiences in the United

Bob Marley and the Wailers perform for a BBC concert in 1973, the year in which the band began to enjoy international success.

States, Great Britain, and elsewhere. To soften the beat, Blackwell added extra lead guitar and keyboard tracks. To catch the consumers' eye, he packaged the album in a jacket that looked like a metal Zippo cigarette lighter on which the top opened up to reveal the record.

Even as *The Harder They Come* was exposing the world to reggae, however, *Catch a Fire* did not sell very well. Yet for many reasons, Blackwell refused to stop promoting Marley, as Timothy White explains in *Catch Fire: The Life of Bob Marley*:

> Blackwell believed that Marley was the only figure in Jamaica remotely capable of having a lasting impact on mainstream popular music, the only one with the charisma to back up his atypical talent. As for the [mystical] Rasta message threaded through the riddim, it would have to take care of itself—just as it always had.
>
> Only a Jamaican would be eccentric enough to conceive of such a campaign. Only an Englishman would be arrogant enough to try to execute it. Only an unreconstructed misfit with cash to bash would have the free time to bother. Blackwell filled the bill. Like Marley, he was his own brand of eerie hybrid.[62]

Reggae International

Marley recorded *Burnin'*, his last album with Bunny Wailer and Peter Tosh, in 1973. Unlike *Catch a Fire*, this album attracted international notice. However, much of the mainstream attention was negative, as *Burnin'* was considered highly controversial. The back cover showed Marley smoking a huge "spliff," or marijuana cigarette, as big as a soda bottle. The inside cover of the album showed scenes of Kingston ghettos and Jamaicans, old and young, wearing long, snaky dreadlocks. The incendiary songs on the album, such as "Get Up, Stand Up," "Burnin' and Lootin'," and especially "I Shot the Sheriff," were also considered revolutionary. Timothy White elaborates:

> A lot of people believe that [an African] cult of demonically anti-white murderers had been uncovered in the Caribbean. The music conjured up images of white tourists being hacked to death on the fringes of tropical golf courses. . . . The American press, which had been napping when *Catch A Fire* appeared, now began running long, detailed pieces on this Jamaican cult that [bowed] in front of icons of an Ethiopian despot [Haile Selassie] and smoked more pot than the [hippie] populations of Haight-Ashbury and Greenwich Village combined.[63]

While the attention was negative, it elevated Marley to a godlike status in Jamaica and other poverty-stricken countries in the Caribbean and Africa. Marley did not gain the attention of a mainstream audience, however, until 1975, when English rock star Eric Clapton covered "I Shot the Sheriff."

An Assassination Attempt

By 1976, Bob Marley was so popular and influential that he had unwillingly become a political figure in Jamaica. During a violent and closely fought election, leaders of both the country's political parties felt that an endorsement by Marley would ensure their victory. Marley refused to take sides but was asked to headline a concert for national unity called "Smile Jamaica," sponsored by Jamaica's Socialist prime minister Michael Manley. After receiving a guarantee that the concert would be nonpolitical, Marley reluctantly agreed to play. This was seen as a tacit endorsement of Manley, and the death threats from the right-wing opposition party started immediately.

Marley surrounded his house with a group of vigilante security guards, but on December 3, they disappeared. Moments later, two carloads of gunmen drove into the yard and opened fire on the house with automatic weapons. Marley's manager, Don Taylor, was shot five times; Rita Marley took one bullet to the head; and Bob was shot twice. Miraculously, no one was killed and everyone eventually recovered.

Two days later, Marley performed a ninety-minute set at the "Smile Jamaica" concert in front of eighty thousand cheering fans. As he stood onstage he was protected by two hundred supporters who surrounded him. At one point, he opened up his shirt and pointed to his chest and arm wounds, pulled out two imaginary guns to shoot, then pointed his thumbs up. The experience left Marley hurt, disillusioned, and bitter. He and his family spent the next fourteen months living in exile in London.

The song reached number one on the American pop charts and—twelve years after his first record with the Wailers—Bob Marley's stunning talent was suddenly recognized by an international array of critics and fans.

During this period Marley released the albums *Natty Dread, Live!*, and *Rastaman Vibration*. These records were extremely influential, as Gilmore attests in his authoritative profile in *Rolling Stone*:

> Like the milestone albums of the Beatles, Bob Dylan, Jimi Hendrix, the Rolling Stones, Marvin Gaye and Sly Stone, these were records that created new sonic ground and

changed how we would hear music. They were also albums that announced Marley as a pre-eminent musical figure. Though his music during this time didn't sell millions, he was quickly seen to possess a creative brilliance and fearless integrity. In short, Bob Marley became a considerable and widely recognized force, and numerous other artists during the 1970s—from Paul McCartney and Stevie Wonder to Elvis Costello and the Police—would reflect his influence by following through on some of the possibilities that his music was creating.[64]

With Marley's ascension into the rock pantheon, Jamaican music was finally a worldwide sensation. Other artists, such as Burning Spear, the Abyssinians, the Itals, and Big Youth were also able to find success among reggae-hungry consumers. Around this time the genre came to be known as 'roots' reggae. The term *roots* applied to songs with lyrics that were concerned with several topics, including the suffering of people in the ghetto, Haile Selassie as a black messiah, slavery in "Babylon," repatriation to Africa, and other Rastafarian concepts. Meanwhile Marley, ever faithful to his Rastafarian beliefs, continued to spread the roots message of justice, equality, and peace.

Marley's Death and Legacy

Marley would not find peace, however. In 1976 he survived an assassination attempt while trying to broker a cease-fire between Jamaica's warring political gangs. The next year he injured his toe playing soccer. The wound refused to heal. A London doctor warned that if the toe was not amputated, it would turn cancerous. Rastafarians are forbidden to undergo amputation, however, and Marley refused surgery. Unfortunately cancer did develop in the injured toe and, by 1980, had spread to Marley's brain. On May 11, 1981, the thirty-six-year-old musician, already a legend, died in Miami. His body was flown to Jamaica for a state funeral. The government declared the day May 20 a national day of mourning and twelve thousand people viewed Marley's body in the Kingston National Arena. Another ten thousand gathered outside. Thousands more lined the roads on the way to Nine Mile, waiting for a glimpse of the pickup truck that bore the coffin.

Marley's death ended an era in Jamaican music. While roots reggae is still played in Jamaica, no other musician has ever reached the level of fame Marley achieved. His message of resistance, freedom, and justice is still heard in other performance styles, especially rap. Marley's gift, however, was to wrap the harsh realities of racism and the revolutionary message of liberation in sweet-sounding melodies and catchy arrangements. As Chang and Chen write: "Bob's splendid talent for melody remained with him throughout [his career] and made even his most preachifying and didactic [morally instructive] songs danceable and singable."[65]

Bob Marley salutes the crowd with a raised fist during a 1978 concert in Sweden. Today, Marley's music continues to inspire millions of people.

In June 1975, as if somehow knowing that he would not have a long life, Marley told an interviewer, "My music will go on forever,"[66] and these words are proving to be true. When *Songs of Freedom*, a four-CD boxed set of Marley's life work, was released in 1992, it sold more than a million copies the first year. That year, over twenty-five thousand people visited the Marley Museum in his old headquarters in Jamaica. *Legend*, Marley's greatest hits album, first issued in 1984, still sells about a million copies a year.

Marley's fame continues into the twenty-first century. *Time* magazine chose his album *Exodus* as one of the best albums of the twentieth century, and after his death the reggae master was given a star on Hollywood Boulevard and a Grammy

Lifetime Achievement Award in 2001. The 1977 video *Bob Marley Live at the Rainbow*, in London, was enclosed in a time capsule to be opened in the year 3000. There is little doubt that Marley would have taken such honors in stride. He often told interviewers that he cared little for money or fame, stating in October 1975: "Money is not my richness. My richness is to live and walk on the earth barefoot."[67]

Roots reggae, the music Marley introduced to the world, has influenced bands ranging from the Beatles and the Talking Heads to newer groups such as Rancid, Smashmouth, and 311. And, on the island, as ever, the music changes and grows as new generations of West Kingston youth transform reggae into something new, something different, and something uniquely Jamaican.

Chapter Five

Dub, Toasting, and Dancehall

In the 1970s, Bob Marley traveled the world introducing roots reggae to audiences in Africa, Europe, the United States, and elsewhere. Even as Rastafarian reggae was becoming a worldwide phenomenon, back in Jamaica, artists making homegrown music continued to experiment with different techniques and sounds. Moving away from the roots reggae genre, producers aimed at creating commercial music for sound system lawns and dancehalls. A new style called "dub" emerged. Like most other Jamaican style trends, dub recycled material from the past and blended them with new elements to create a new sound.

Dub is defined simply as a remix of a popular song. In Jamaica, this remix, or "version," generally had the singing removed, the bass and drums turned up louder than on the original, and new tracks added. At first, dubbing or versioning was simply a way to make new tracks for sound system lawns; but as producers grew more creative and in-

ventive, dub became an art form unto itself.

A Spine-Tingling Moment

Jamaican dub can trace its birth to 1967, when a record manufacturer accidentally pressed the previously released Paragons single "On the Beach" without the vocal track. The record presser, known only as Smith, gave the instrumental single to a deejay named Ruddy Redwood. That night Redwood played the dub track back-to-back with the vocal version. Within seconds, the crowd began singing the familiar song along with the dub, a moment described by Bradley in *Bass Culture*:

> [According] to those who were there, it was a totally spine-tingling moment when the whole point of the island's music business thus far made perfect sense. Imagine it: it's a warm night; Ruddy Redwood, known as Mr. Midnight because he begins spinning tunes at pre-

cisely that time, comes on to a nicely loosened crowd, and although that instrumental cut must have surprised everybody, within seconds they have claimed it for their own and are joining in. Music made by the people for the people, unique in this respect to Jamaica's sound systems.[68]

Redwood continued to play the dub "On the Beach," and the crowd sang along all night. The next day, the event was brought to the attention of producer Duke Reid, who immediately began remixing some of the dozens of hits he had produced in his Treasure Isle studios. While simply dropping the vocals worked well for the sound system crowds,

Deejay U-Roy talks over a dub track during a performance. Many music historians credit U-Roy as the first rap artist.

Reid loved American rhythm and blues and so began adding hot R&B–style lead guitar and organ solos to the versions. Within a year, Reid's success spawned many imitators, and most of Jamaica's record producers began dubbing their hits into instrumentals.

U-Roy Toasts to Dub

Dub entered another critical phase in 1970 when deejay U-Roy (Ewart Beckford) entered the Treasure Isle studios and began talking over a dub of the Techniques' "You Don't Care for Me at All." This technique, known as "toasting," had U-Roy shouting exclamations similar to those he used at sound system dances. U-Roy describes his toasting style: "You feel the vibe of the music and you make certain talk . . . and you say whatever you feel like saying, you know?"[69] When U-Roy's version of "You Don't Care for Me at All" was burned on a dubplate and taken to a sound system dance that night, U-Roy toasted live over his toasting on the record and the crowd went wild. U-Roy's precedent-setting single became an instant hit. While it remained a local phenomenon, it is acknowledged as the first rap music ever recorded. The deejay comments on this historical event:

> I never thought anything too big was going to come from [my records]. And now people are rapping and doing that kind of stuff, so it's like, 'Man this is really exciting!' . . . And it's an honour for me to know that I started something, or I

did something that people appreciated so much that other people would imitate it, you know what I mean? I don't have a problem with that. I'm just happy for all the rappers and DJs or whatever it might be.[70]

U-Roy quickly went back into the studio and toasted over two more instrumentals, "Waken the Town (and Tell the People)" and "(This Station) Rules the Nation." With "You Don't Care for Me at All," the rapping deejay soon had the top three records on the Jamaican charts. After this success, nearly every hit produced in Jamaican recording studios was accompanied by a dub version with no vocals and a deejay version with rap. Often the deejay version would have the original vocals turned louder and softer, with the deejay adding his toast between lyrics. This created an exciting "joust" between the singer and the deejay.

By 1972 U-Roy, the original rapper, had a host of imitators. Foremost among them was Dennis Alcapone, who was in such demand for his talents that three established producers—Duke Reid, Coxsone, and Bunny Lee—all produced records with him in a short period of time. Alcapone flooded the market with his records, and the song "Deejay's Choice" was the first of many to brag about the deejay phenomenon. On the single, Alcapone toasts the greatness of his contemporaries Big Youth, U-Roy, and I Roy, even imitating their distinctive vocal styles.

U-Roy's Original Rap

Although many believe rap originated in America's inner-city neighborhoods, the first rapper was Jamaican deejay Ewart Beckford, known as U-Roy. Chris Yurkiw explains in his "Like a Version" Web article:

U-Roy wasn't the first Jamaican "deejay" to both play records and chat freestyle over the music—advertisements, sound-system IDs, or whatever party banter that would come into his head. . . . But U-Roy, [whose real name is] Ewart Beckford . . . was the first to take his dancehall flow into the studio and lay it down on wax. He would just toast right on top of an already-recorded hit, over the instrumental bits, [and] voilà deejay music went legit in late '60s Jamaica, and rap had its O.G.—original godfather.

Admittedly, U-Roy's old "rapping" is a far cry from what we now know in the institution of hip hop, but it's not a great leap from his talking over songs to early hip hop hits like "Rapper's Delight"—basically rapping over the backing track of Chic's "Good Times"—or even latter-day stuff like Coolio's "Gangsta's Paradise," the base of which is a macro-sample of a Stevie Wonder song. And hip hop historians know all too well that one of the first Bronx rap DJs was Cool Herc, a Jamaican émigré.

U-Roy's rap style was eventually heard in the United States in the mid-1970s, when deejay Cool Herc, a Jamaican emigrant, began hauling his turntables and sound system to the parks in New York City and the Bronx. When giving free concerts in the parks, Cool Herc did not utilize complete songs. Instead the deejay chose to play the funkiest parts from his records. To do so, he developed techniques such as "needle dropping," starting a song at a specific passage, and "backspinning," playing the record backward with his finger.

These innovations quickly became central to hip-hop, a musical style that was further developed by Grandmaster Flash and other American rappers.

The King Tubby Treatment

Even before the hip-hop phenomenon, dub entered a third phase in Jamaica in 1972 when Osbourne Ruddock, known as King Tubby, used his engineering talents to create a new sound. At that time, King Tubby owned Tubby's Home Town HiFi, one of the premier sound systems in Kingston. Tubby employed U-Roy as a deejay and was the first sound system operator to use electronic effects such as echo and reverb. The sound is described by Alcapone:

> When King Tubby had a sound system . . . I never hear nothing like it in my whole life. . . . Tubby had him steel horns [speakers] for the treble and he put them up in the trees so it's like the sound is coming from all over. . . . They had reverb on that sound system, no other sound system had reverb at the time—Tubby was the one who introduce it. . . . His bass was so round and fat that every singer sound wonderful, every song sound *rich*. . . . And the echo was another thing, nobody else had that, either. When U-Roy used to take up the mic [microphone] to start his session and say, "Now this commence up the *night . . . night . . . night . . . night. . .*", the people would go wild.[71]

Tubby used the same tricks in the studio, cutting versions with U-Roy toasting over heavy echo and reverb. As the only producer using these effects, Tubby all but eliminated competition for a time. Dub versions of records released with credits saying "King Tubby's Version" or "Drums & Bass by King Tubby's"[72] became instant number-one hits regardless of the vocal version on the other side of the single. His competition even brought their songs to the studio to get the so-called Tubby treatment.

Grandmaster Flash, a pioneer hip-hop deejay, refined sound-system techniques such as backspinning on turntables and needle dropping.

King Tubby's Studio Wizardry

King Tubby is an electronics genius who reinvented the recording studio in the early 1970s. Deejay Mikey Cambell, also known as Mikey Dread, describes Tubby's wizardry in Bass Culture *by Lloyd Bradley:*

The man invented a whole heap of things and don't get no credit. He made his first echo machine with two old tape recorders. He built spring-loaded switches for his sound effects, so it's pressure-sensitive and he can hit it hard or soft or slowly to get a different sound from each effect like a thunder clap or an explosion. He would figure out an effect he wanted, then design and construct the circuit that would give him that. . . . An' he just play with things that people make, too. He customize his Fisher reverb unit until the factory wouldn't recognize it; in fact, not much of his equipment stayed the way it was when it come out the factory. Such was his knowledge that if the man don't think a sound is like how he want it, he would go into the circuitry there and then and change it to create the particular effect that he want. . . . Plus he worked hard. Even when he not actually at the board, he still working [because he's] thinking about things or trying new things out or reading a book or just practicing— like the great musicians practice all the time, so did King Tubby. He knew he had to, and nobody out there could keep up with him.

Tubby worked his musical magic in a studio that was as unique as the sounds produced there. In an era before sophisticated recording equipment was available in Jamaica, Tubby used his knowledge of electronics to create his own systems, building multitrack recorders that allowed him to mix 4 tracks onto a single record. (By comparison, modern computerized recording systems have at least 128 tracks.)

When not making number one hits, he often spent his time building and re-building new gear in his tiny studio located behind his mother's house in West Kingston. Bradley describes the situation:

As a result of its owner's professional expertise in electronic theory, his phenomenal effectiveness with a soldering iron and his uncanny ability to see beyond the music on the tape, King Tubby's Studio was in an almost organic state of affairs. . . . [It] was a perpetually evolving state of the art, morphing into whatever the master required as he added equipment, added—and bastardized—new outboard gear and tinkered with the circuitry on an almost daily basis.[73]

While Tubby was the king of versions, there were others who followed his lead, including Prince Jammy, Prince Phillip Smart, and the Scientist. Dub producer ET was an innovator who attained great popularity using backward vocals and singing recorded at slow speeds. Established producers such as Lee Perry, Prince Buster, and Coxsone also added their creativity to the dub boom, incorporating sounds such as recording tape being rewound or thunder claps made by pounding a fist down onto the spring-loaded reverb unit, which then produced a loud crashing noise.

The Dub Poets

The dub phenomenon ran parallel to the international rise of reggae. While many deejays were happy to toast to apolitical topics, a new breed of rapper, labeled dub poets, emerged. These poets blended the political stance of reggae with the toasting traditions of dub. This style grew in popularity in the second half of the 1970s, when Jamaica was gripped by bloody political and gang violence. In *Solid Foundation*, Katz describes the characteristics of dub poetry: "Dub poetry stems from the experimental setting of verse to music: the politically challenging poems, often expounding a Rastafari world view, are typically recited in a heavy patois, whilst the rhythmic emphasis is provided by straightforward reggae or a backdrop of jazzy instrumentals and [traditional Rastafarian drumming]."[74]

Dub poets are distinguished from deejays in several ways. They are poets first, not entertainers who rap at sound system dances, and they speak their verse only over reggae dub tracks. While deejays might sometimes make political comments, dub poets tend to deal with serious, complex topics, such as gang violence and the persistence of poverty in the developing world.

Dub poets are also distinguished from toasting deejays by the distinct reggae rhythm not only in the backing music but also in the words. The man credited with inventing dub poetry, Oku Onoura, explains, saying dub poetry is not simply a matter of "putting a piece of poem [on top of] a reggae rhythm; it is a poem that has a built-in reggae rhythm backing, one can distinctly hear the reggae rhythm coming out of the poem."[75]

Among dub poets, Mutabaruka has had the most commercial success. Mutabaruka, whose name means "one who is always victorious" in a Rwandan tribal language, began his career by publishing his poems in the music magazine *Reggae Swing*. After performing in literary circles, he began making intelligent and passionate records in the mid-1970s. Mutabaruka describes his work:

> Most of what I write is what I feel and what I see. I learned that the pen is sometimes mightier than the

Mutabaruka is the best-known voice of the new wave of dub poets, who deal with serious social issues.

A Return to the Dancehall

While dub poets chanted their words over roots reggae versions, another twist on dub hit Jamaica in the late 1970s. This style, known as dancehall, began with live vocalists singing over dub versions at sound system events. A sound system promoter named Sugar Minott is credited with this innovation. Minott had a sound system called Youthman Promotion that played dances throughout Kingston. Minott and other select vocalists would pick up a microphone and sing to the rhythm tracks that, ironically, had been scrubbed of their original vocals in the studio. These productions were the first to be called dancehall music.

The term *dancehall* did not come into popular use until 1983 when a company called Inner City Promotions held a show at a drive-in theater. This event, called Dancehall 83, featured toasting deejays along with singers performing over dub versions. Jamaican music columnist Howard McGowan recalls the scene: "The particular manner in which this event was marketed caught the attention of the downtowners, the real dance goers, and it almost flattened the venue. A massive crowd turned out, and those of us with experience in the business knew a chord had been struck."[77]

sword and people can write things and motivate people to think; that is what my work is all about, to make you think. When you listen to my poems . . . it must motivate you to find solutions for your problems. I cannot guarantee to have all the solutions to all of the problems, but I can make you think of the problems and be motivated towards a constructive solution.[76]

In the years that followed, dancehall was not only a word used to define the places where dances were held. The word was also used to describe the type of music that was performed there and the entire culture that attended dancehall events. By the mid-1980s, the role of vocalists diminished while the deejay remained king of the Jamaican dancehall.

The primary difference between the dancehall genre and dub was the focus of the lyrics. In 1980, with the defeat of Socialist prime minister Michael Manley by the record producer turned right-wing politician Edward Seaga, Jamaica made a turn toward the conservative politics that would dominate the decade. Barrow and Dalton discuss how this political trend affected dancehall music:

In reaction, the island's music became conservative and inward look-

Dances and Dancehall Music

For a dancehall song to become a hit, it needed an infectious rhythm that inspired people to dance. Producers often looked to dancers themselves to find ideas for building new rhythms in the studio. In Reggae: The Story of Jamaican Music, *deejays Burru Banton, Flourgon, and Reggie Steppers discuss how dancers inspire new rhythms and how beats inspire new dance steps:*

Burru: In Jamaica, we keep changing our style of dancing and then the rhythms will be changed a little to suit it, like if people started moving double time or something. [But] then when completely new rhythms appear somebody will start a dance to go with it.

Reggie: They go together most of the time, or nobody can tell which came first [the rhythm or the dance]. The Bogle dance came out just after the rhythm. Buju play the tune first, then the dance appear. . . .

Flourgon: What about the [dance called the] Giggy? That was a rhythm created . . . because somebody was insane—there was a madman dancing down at [the club] Crossroads and a producer went down there, watch him dance and he built a rhythm right after and that's how the Giggy came about.

Burru: If some artist see a little youth doing a dance in the dancehall and he like the dance he may copy it and sing a song about it. Another artist may then change the name of that dance to something that suit a lyric that he's already doing and it might take off that way, so one thing can become another.

ing. The reliance on tried and tested rhythms became more pronounced, while lyrics tend to turn away from social, political or historical themes. Now the emphasis shifted to traditional dancehall concerns—new dance moves [and] slackness (sexually explicit lyrics).[78]

Dancehall was also musically different from dub. In the 1970s, the strength of a dub hit was usually based on the power of the rhythm, which had been used on a previously popular song. The chattering of the deejays simply added to the song's impact. In the 1980s the popularity of a dancehall deejay was primarily based on his words, not on the rhythm tracks. In competition for the ears of the audience, those who could come up with the most boastful or humorous raps were in the greatest demand. This was most obvious in "slack" lyrics, which treated women as sexual objects and glorified the deejays themselves as men who were well endowed both financially and sexually.

The Dancehall Massive

Dancehall meant more than just toasting and music to the average Jamaican. In fact dancehall was, and remains, a way of life, and is the most popular cultural pastime in Jamaica. The crowds who attend dancehall events, called the dancehall massive, influence life in Jamaica, and sometimes the world over, with their styles of clothing, haircuts, jewelry, and dance. Dancehall culture has even affected the Jamaican language as deejays invent new words and phrases nearly every night.

In the mid-1980s, as slack deejays took over the dancehalls, women's fashion was influenced by the sexually explicit music. As Norman C. Stolzoff writes in *Wake the Town and Tell the People*:

Many female dancehall fans stopped wearing the modest "rootsy" styles dictated by Rastafari-inspired gender codes and started donning flashy, revealing outfits, especially when they attended dances in the urban environs of Kingston. . . . These dancehall "divas," as they came to be called, pushed even further by designing and wearing "X-rated, bare as you dare" costumes to dances. . . . The body was now a site of increasing degrees of adornment. These "donnettes" demonstrated their physical and financial "ass-ets" by wearing clothes labeled "batty riders," [defined] as "a skirt or pair of shorts which expose more of the buttocks than it conceals." . . . Wigs of all colors, mesh tops, large jewelry (gold bangles, rings, earrings, nose rings), and elaborate hairdos all became part of the new fashion ensemble. Men's dancehall fashions changed as well, shifting from the hippie and African inspired garb of the roots era to flashy suits, abundant jewelry, and hairdos made popular by American rappers. Unlike the women, however, male dancehall fans and performers

Dressed in a provocative outfit, a dancehall girl does the splits while standing on her head on the dance floor.

continued to cover their bodies in long, draping outfits that hid rather than revealed their shape.[79]

Some women joined fashion "posses" that competed against one another by donning the most outrageous clothing. Eventually, this informal rivalry was transformed by models and fashion industry insiders into formal fashion competitions. As deejays blasted out versions

and toasted, women paraded in competition for the title of dancehall queen.

Dances were also changing in the sexually charged dancehall atmosphere. A move known as "bubbling" was performed by men and women who circled their hips in a tight rotation. The dancehall queen Carlene Smith popularized the acrobatic "head dancing," which involved dancing on the head while keeping the feet on the ground.

Such antics performed by the dancehall massive were breathlessly covered in the Jamaican media, adding further legitimacy to dancehall culture. Specialty magazines such as *X-News* catered to dancehall culture and the radio station IRIE FM played dancehall music. Beyond these outlets, the nation's largest-circulation newspaper, *the Gleaner*, printed dancehall news, and events were even covered on the television channel CVM-TV.

Mister Yellowman

Ironically, as fashion and beauty became more important, a man with a genetic condition that had made him an outcast most of his life became Jamaica's top

The dancehall deejay superstar Yellowman capitalized on his albinism and developed a brash improvisational style of toasting.

superstar deejay. Born Winston Foster in 1959, the performer originally known as Yellowman is an albino with yellow hair, very light skin, and pink eyes. His childhood was fraught with hardships as his albinism made him the focus of cruel taunts and violent bullies. While enduring hostility for his appearance, Yellowman developed a bold, cocky toasting style. After winning a Kingston talent contest in 1979, he went on to delight crowds all over Jamaica with his swaggering, boastful, and often comical improvised lyrics. Working with a sound system based in neighboring St. Thomas, Yellowman drew huge audiences to his dancehall performances and for a time was as popular in Jamaica as Marley had been.

The island's producers were eager to work with this dancehall phenomenon, and King Yellow, as he came to be known, released up to five albums a year. Yellowman's improvisational style worked well for him in the studio, as he comments: "If you good, you know, you have lyrics come straight to you. . . . Most of the lyrics I do on record, is in the studio I mek them up. . . . [Producer Henry "Junjo" Lawes] just call me an' say I must do an album, and I just listen to the rhythms and the lyrics come to me."[80]

The 1982 album *Mister Yellowman* helped launch the toaster to international fame and is considered to be one of his best. On tracks such as "Morning Ride," which became a dancehall anthem, Yellowman chants and sings over stripped-down backing tracks consisting mostly of prominent bass, light drums, and low, volume guitar chords swathed in special effects, such as reverb and echo. This sound, with the heavy bass and lyrics as the primary tracks, came to dominate the dancehall style.

The Singjay Style

As with other Jamaican stars, Yellowman had plenty of competition in the dancehall. Foremost among them was the comically named Eek-A-Mouse, born Ripton Joseph Hylton in 1957. At 6 feet 6 inches tall (1.98m), Eek-A-Mouse has a highly charged stage presence, and his elastic face is known for its manic expressions. He delights crowds with his unique vocal technique known as "singjay," or singjay, a style that is neither singing nor deejaying, but a mix of the two. The singjay style is embellished with often bizarre drumlike sounds. The vocal styling of Mouse is described by the *Washington Post*: "With a voice that's the stuff of children's nightmares, and often seems to have a life of its own, he squeaks, squawks, bing-bing-bings and dem-di-dems ad infinitum."[81]

Working with Yellowman producer Junjo Lawes in 1982, Eek-A-Mouse created a host of smash singles from the seminal album *Wa Do Dem* including "Wild Like a Tiger," "For Hire and Removal," "Do You Remember," and "Ganja Smuggling." Although he moved to southern California in the 1990s, he continues to perform. A 2005 tour took the singjay style to Europe as Mouse played dates in Germany, the Netherlands, Sweden, and Denmark.

Slackness Rules

Those who tried to compete with Eek-A-Mouse and Yellowman were required to be as inventive—or shocking—as possible. By the late 1980s, deejays were able to garner the most attention by using slack lyrics to excite increasingly jaded dancehall audiences. Like rap in the United States, some deejays also celebrated explicit violence, misogyny, and homophobia.

By the mid-1980s, the politically charged roots reggae of Marley had been transformed into a sound that oc-cupied an entirely different place in the social spectrum. Like Marley, however, its creators grew up in the Kingston ghetto, and found popularity by putting to music the incidents of their daily lives. In *Reggae: The Story of Jamaican Music*, Bradley gives perspective to this sea change:

> Immediately prior to dancehall, roots reggae's success had been remarkable. Way beyond merely Marley, [roots reggae groups such as] Third World, Black Uhuru, Culture

Black Uhuru performs onstage with the Police in 1982. At the same time as reggae music became an international phenomenon in the 1980s, slack music rose to prominence in Jamaica.

and Burning Spear had become internationally acknowledged, signed to major record deals and made albums for world consumption. . . . [As] a result their priorities and considerations were becoming far less parochial. It was as if roots reggae didn't really belong to the home crowd any longer, and therefore was becoming increasingly less relevant. . . . [Then] there was the feeling among the [sufferer] classes that 10 years of beating down Babylon hadn't achieved an awful lot. The time had come to dance to a different beat, one controlled [by the poor folks] downtown.[82]

Some might even argue that the musical contributions of the "downtown" deejays were as important as those of Marley. While reggae is still enjoyed by millions, rap is the dominant popular music of the twenty-first century. Without U-Roy, Yellowman, and dozens of others, rap might never have evolved into the worldwide phenomenon it is today.

Chapter Six

Ragga and Reggae Worldwide

In the 1980s, dancehall music consisted of deejays rapping over dub tracks about sex, dancing, and gangster life. While the style remained popular throughout the decade, it was given an entirely new sound in 1985 when a new generation of digital music technology was introduced on Jamaica. The drum machines, digital keyboards, digital recorders, and other computerized gadgets were primitive by current standards but fomented a revolution in reggae nonetheless.

The sound of dancehall reggae played entirely with digital instruments came to be known as ragga reggae (from *raggamuffin*, a term previously applied to poverty-stricken ghetto youth in Jamaica). Featuring stars such as Shabba Ranks, Red Dragon, Cobra, and Terror Fabulous, ragga was the most commercially successful Jamaican music since the roots reggae sound of Bob Marley in the late 1970s.

As with earlier genres of Jamaican music, economics played a part in the development of ragga. Digital recording and the introduction of CDs as a music format lowered the cost of making records and allowed producers not only to experiment with untested rhythms but also to put out hundreds of albums a year. Leading the way was producer King Jammy, formerly Prince Jammy, who kicked the digital revolution into high gear virtually overnight.

Digital Jamaica

In 1985, Jammy programmed a digital Casio Music Box keyboard to record a rhythm track on the song "Under Me Sleng Teng." The basic rhythm, with no bass and few frills, was accompanied by Wayne Smith's improvised words praising ganja. In *Reggae: The Story of Jamaican Music*, Lloyd Bradley elaborates:

The buzzsaw-like drone of the delivery redefined "rudimentary." But the result was so compelling a piece of music that for several months (a lifetime in reggae's accelerated

Ragga and Reggae Worldwide **83**

Record producers gather around King Jammy's customized recording equipment, with which Jammy produced scores of albums.

timescale) it became something of a challenge to walk around without hearing the "Sleng Teng" rhythm in your head, a situation not helped by the fact that it was blaring out of cars, shops, open windows and radios every few yards.[83]

Although the Casio would be considered a toy in the twenty-first century, "Sleng Teng" was the first time a digital drum track appeared on a Jamaican record. The response was incredible. Within weeks, the song had been dubbed in more than a hundred different versions. Jammy himself put out two entire albums of the track and nearly every producer on the island followed with their own version of "Sleng Teng."

In the years that followed "Sleng Teng," Jammy kept up an incredible pace, producing at least 150 albums during the next five years. His success spawned a host of rivals who were able to get into the production business because of the dramatically lowered cost provided by digital recording equipment.

With the introduction of digital recording, nearly every old song was reworked with programmed drum tracks, strange audio effects, and other digital sounds. Old riddims from ska and rocksteady classics such as "Bam Bam," "Fire Burning," and "Oh Carolina" were reworked with computerized keyboards and drums.

Digitized music was also able to move out of the studio and make a splash directly at sound system venues. While some continued to record in the studio, ponderous soundboards, complicated multitrack tape recorders, and expensive keyboards were history. Deejays could simply take their computers to sound system lawns and create customized sounds to fit the mood of the dancers. As Bradley writes:

> Characters like Brigadier Jerry, Ranking Joe and Fat Head may have got record deals, but there was a whole host of others who could

Innovative Rhythms from the "Riddim Twins"

Two of the leading innovators in digital reggae, Sly Dunbar and Robbie Shakespeare, have a musical foundation in roots reggae. Bassist Shakespeare played with Bob Marley, and he and drummer Dunbar both worked with Peter Tosh from the original Wailers. In the late 1970s they put their talents together, and their innovative dancehall rhythms earned them the nickname the "Riddim Twins."

In the early 1980s their unique rhythms became the leading sound of ragga. Dunbar used the synthesizing equipment called Syndrums to produce a drum sound that was described as metallic and robotic, but set the digital reggae revolution into motion. Forming their own record label, Taxi, Sly and Robbie pioneered original sounds with Black Uhuru, the Wailing Souls, and Gregory Isaacs. They also produced a series of hot instrumental records with their band the Taxi Gang. Their work caught the attention of international stars such as Bob Dylan, Grace Jones, and Mick Jagger of the Rolling Stones, who used the Riddim Twins on their albums. By the early 1990s, the successful rhythm duo were producing nearly half of the number-one songs recorded in Jamaica.

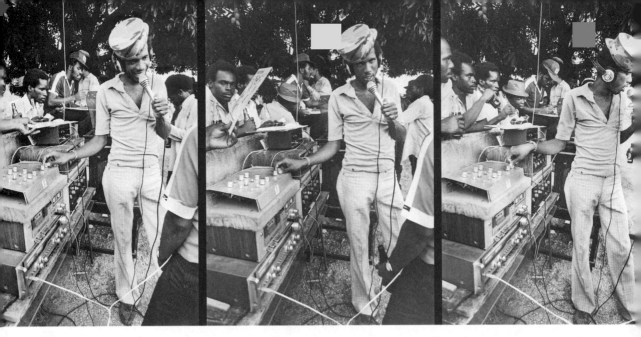

A dancehall deejay uses his equipment to tailor his music to suit the mood of the crowd. Such equipment allowed deejays to create customized sounds.

make themselves heard . . . as they'd simply take up a mic [microphone] at a sound system and rock the crowd. Once again there was virtually no difference between the artists and the audiences, and the rank and file grabbed their chance to participate with both hands. Talent flooded in and the art of deejaying became more and more . . . progressive. . . . It was these street-level, more spontaneous deejays who pushed the producers into delving deeper and deeper into their new computers to find evermore challenging backing tracks. Which in turn inspired the microphone masters to greater heights.[84]

Hardcore Dancehall

By the end of the 1980s, increasingly sophisticated digital drums, samplers, synthesizers, and other equipment were changing the sound of ragga music as producers used the new tools to weave densely layered digital rhythms with traditional sounds. According to Stolzoff, producers

drew on the rhythms of Pocomania and Kumina [Pukumina], two Afro-Jamaican sacred forms, and musical forms such as mento and burru. The distinctive drum pattern, two-chord melodies, and electronic overdubs of these songs have become the distinguished markers of what is referred to as 'hardcore dancehall,' as distinct from early dancehall-style musical arrangements that [were not elaborately produced but] used live musicians in the studio.[85]

The lyrics recited by the hardcore dancehall deejays increasingly began dealing with violent topics, generating considerable controversy. In a shift away from the sexual braggadocio of slackness, "gun songs," or "gun lyrics," use vivid and explicit imagery to describe the shocking brutality in parts of Kingston where hundreds are murdered every year.

The popularity of gun songs increased in the late 1980s when drug dealers in Peru and Colombia began using Jamaica as a central transshipment station for cocaine on its way to the United States. The drug flooded into Kingston's ghettos, followed by murder and mayhem as hundreds of young men formed violent drug cartels, some of them international in scope. According to a 1993 *Billboard* magazine article by Maureen Sheridan, these developments were reflected in "a musical switch from marijuana-influenced acoustic reggae to the cocaine-charged computer beat of dancehall, where acts with names like Bounty Killer and Destruction have replaced those of more cultural [focus], such as the Abyssinians, Burning Spear, and Culture."[86] In this atmosphere, guns were increasingly prevalent at sound system events. Some fans showed their enthusiasm for the music, or their disapproval, by firing guns into the air, a practice known as a "lick shot."

These potentially lethal activities at the dancehall drew the attention of the government, which moved to ban gun

Hardcore dancehall deejays like Bounty Killer glorified the violence of gangster life with songs containing explicitly brutal lyrics.

songs, especially those that glorified the murderous ways of gangsters. Since there is no constitutional right to free speech in Jamaica, performers could expect such songs to be declared illegal. Former Jamaican police commissioner Trevor McMillan cites the Jamaica Act: "Whosoever shall solicit, encourage, persuade, or endeavor to persuade . . . any person to murder any other person . . . shall be guilty of a misdemeanor and liable to a sentence not exceeding 10 years with or without hard labor." Thus he contends, "Some dancehall lyrics are in breach of the laws in Jamaica. . . . I am not trying to legislate morality, but there is a difference between freedom of expression and irresponsibly breaking the law."[87]

Unsurprisingly, official opposition and threats of imprisonment served to increase the popularity of gun lyrics. Any deejay who wanted to burnish his image as a tough gangster only had to thumb his nose at authority by reciting explicitly brutal lyrics. And while many traditional reggae musicians bemoaned this new violent musical trend, some critics compared the gun-song genre favorably to the roots reggae tradition. As Ben Thielen writes in "The Change of Messages in Dancehall" Web article:

> This shift of attention from a global or continental struggle to describing life in one's neighborhood has brought this form of expression considerable criticism. . . . [Outsiders] to the culture of ragga tend to find these narratives rude [and] crude.

. . . This, however, is what DJs describe as 'strictly reality.' While it can be argued that this reality is lacking sensibility and decency, it should be compared to what the music of roots reggae spoke against. While [the subject of] gun violence [is] certainly grotesque and deplorable . . . [it] conveys a generally unflattering mode of existence. If the listener can get past the vividness of the lyrics of dancehall it quickly becomes apparent that both it and traditional forms of reggae are speaking against social conditions that few of us would care to contend with. The enormous tragedy caused by slavery, colonialism, and despotic rule by an elite class should be considered equally, if not more, morally reprehensible.[88]

Women Artists

As violent rap and sexually explicit lyrics dominated the dancehalls, women artists were scarce in the notoriously sexist Jamaican music scene. In the studios, female vocalists were rarely used for anything but backup singing. A majority of male producers would not even consider recording a woman unless she offered sexual favors in trade. Until the 1990s, there were very few female artists who performed in the dancehalls. The lack of equal opportunity was so blatant that in 1997, Rastafarian attorney Sandra Joy Alcott founded the Jamaica Association of Female Artistes (JAFA) to battle exploitation of women in the record business.

Marcia Griffiths, one of Bob Marley's backup singers, was one of Jamaica's few female musicians to enjoy a solo career.

Alcott describes the situation in *the Jamaica Observer:*

> The horror stories concerning some Jamaican female artistes are numerous, nasty and oftentimes tragic. . . . [No Sex] No Music Deal is a graphic reference to the behaviour of some record producers towards our female artistes. . . . The woman may be courted and may feel that she is in a genuine relationship, only to be cut loose and put to pasture when the man is tired of her and moves on to a next artiste. . . . It may be that a producer may begin to record an artiste, apparently in good faith, and somewhere along the line he begins to 'put questions to her' or to behave in a sexually harassing manner. If she does not give in to these advances, there will be no further recording.[89]

There have been exceptions to this pattern. Marcia Griffiths, one of the I-Threes who sang backup for Bob Marley, had a good career as a solo artist in the reggae era. Following changing trends, Griffiths adopted the ragga style, singing over digital rhythms created by Jamaica's leading producers.

Sex and Lady Saw

Some women have managed to compete with men in the raunchiest of ragga slackness. Deejay Lady Saw (Marion

Lady Saw, notorious for her raunchy dancehall lyrics, provoked some Jamaican government officials to attempt to ban her from performing.

Hall), known as the First Lady of the Dancehall, is famous for her X-rated performances and sexually explicit lyrics. Born in 1972 in the small Jamaican village of St. Mary's, Saw began challenging Jamaica's rudest rude boys in the early 1990s. According to Barrow and Dalton, Saw "gained a reputation for her outrageous sexual boasting —on one record she claims that one man is not enough, but two or three might satisfy her."[90]

Because a sexual double standard exists for women entertainers, the lyrics of Lady Saw generated even more controversy than explicit words recited by men. When she played the music festival Jamaican Sunsplash 1994, a crowd of ten thousand shouted for more. However, her hardcore references to sex generated headlines when several local government officials in Montego Bay moved to permanently ban Lady Saw from performing in Jamaica's second largest city. While the ban was never successful, it generated three months of debate on talk radio shows and on newspaper editorial pages. While Lady Saw argued that she simply was giving the people what they wanted, she also used her talents to mock the attitude of her critics. Believing that the real obscenities were suffered by people whose government was "slack" in fixing problems, she rapped in "What Is Slackness?":

Me [say] society a blame Lady Saw fi [for] de system dem create. . . .

Slackness—is when the road wan' fi fix

Slackness—when the government break dem promise

Slackness when politician issue out guns

So the two party a shoot one another down.[91]

Lady Saw's music caught the attention of Gwen Stefani, lead singer of the American band No Doubt. In 2002 Stefani teamed up with Lady Saw on "Underneath It All," a song that later won a Grammy award.

The continued success of Lady Saw proved that there was room in the Jamaican music business for a female perspective, particularly one that addresses the concerns of women. As Lady Saw states: "I have a lot of female fans because a lot of my songs are defending them. . . . And if men try to put them down, I'll build them up. I'll never put down a woman, and my songs are not cussing them. I'm not doing anything sexual on stage—no raw sex, but I'll talk about it."[92]

Romantic and Cultural Ragga

Not all ragga lyrics have focused on sex and violence. In the 1990s, a subgenre of ragga was popularized by a generation of honey-voiced singers whose lyrics about love were considered old-fashioned by the hardcore crowd. Called romantic ragga, the style is reminiscent of smooth American R&B and is performed by singers such as Sanchez, Thriller, and Mickey Spice. These artists have large female followings in

Reggae Homophobia

Polls show that 96 percent of Jamaicans oppose same-sex marriage, and most are virulently antigay. These sentiments are often expressed in the lyrics of dancehall songs. In 1992 Jamaica's most popular deejay, Buju Banton, had a hit with "Boom Bye Bye," which advocated shooting a homosexual. In Reggae Routes, *Kevin O'Brien Chang and Wayne Chen discuss some of the fallout from the song:*

When "Boom Bye Bye" became a hit in 1992, Buju [Banton] was cementing his status as Jamaica's most popular artist and just beginning to tour abroad. [At the same time] Shabba Ranks had won the first of his Reggae Grammys and had become an almost international star. . . . Then "Boom Bye Byes'" lyrics caught the attention of homosexual groups in America and Britain.

Apparently advocating the killing of homosexuals, the song understandably became embroiled in controversy. *Newsweek* condemned the song as "hatefilled". . . . Sporadic protests began at Buju's concerts, often led by [the militant gay-rights group] ACT UP. Then Shabba Ranks was asked his opinion of the song by a U.K. journalist. He volunteered that he agreed with the song. . . . Suddenly Shabba's concerts started drawing large-scale "gay" protests and pressure from these organizations forced the cancellation of a number of his shows. Shabba at first was unrepentant. But management deemed it prudent for him to apologize and he not only retracted his statements, but agreed to work with gay groups in promoting homosexual tolerance. His concerts were . . . able to proceed in peace. Buju's reaction was the opposite. He continued to condemn homosexuality. His culture did not accept such behavior, he said. Unlike Shabba, his shows continued to be dogged by protests.

Jamaican dancehalls, and sell records internationally as well.

Singer Cocoa Tea, born Calvin Scott in 1959, has been a leading star of romantic ragga. He is also known to inject "cultural," or protest, lyrics reminiscent of roots reggae. The Cocoa Tea Web page describes the singer's style:

Cocoa Tea was one of the few early dancehall stars to carve out a consistent, productive career as the genre evolved over the years. His cool-toned, laid-back vocals were perfect for sweet, smooth lovers rock, and gave him a distinct identity amid his more aggressive peers. Still, he was also capable of toughening up his sound on his cultural protest material, which was often sharply perceptive.[93]

Cocoa Tea scored many hits with love songs, but in 1991 he began to experiment with protest lyrics on the album *Riker's Island*, named after the New York penitentiary where many Jamaican immigrants are imprisoned. On songs such as "Oil Ting" and "No Blood for Oil," the singer stridently opposed the 1991 Gulf War. These controversial songs were banned from radio play in Jamaica and Great Britain.

Shabba Ranks

Cocoa Tea has also joined forces with deejays Shabba Ranks and Home T. on the album *Holding On*, which was a

In 1992 Superstar Shabba Ranks (left) stirred up controversy with antigay remarks. After issuing a public apology, Ranks lost standing with the Jamaican dancehall massive.

major hit in Jamaica with singles such as "Pirates Anthem" and "Who She Love" hitting number one. This blending of soulful singing with deejays best known for their risqué slack lyrics was marked by distinctive beats, catchy lyrics, and state-of-the-art production.

By the time *Holding On* was released, Shabba Ranks was a superstar on the level of Bob Marley in Jamaica, having scored nearly fifty hits, including "Wicked Inna Bed," "Roots and Culture," "Live Blanket," "Mama Man," and "Peeny Peeny." Known for combining rap toasting over reggae rhythms, Shabba was signed by Epic Records in the United States, making him an international star in 1991. His success allowed him to reach a much wider audience than any other Jamaican deejay at the time. The singles that followed appealed to his local fan base with ragga-style songs such as "Ting a Ling," and "Shine & Criss." Meanwhile he enhanced his cultural credentials with political songs "Flag Flown High," "God Bless," and "Heart of a Lion."

In 1992 Shabba gained notoriety for making antigay statements to an interviewer. After protesters began picketing his concerts, the deejay apologized but lost credibility with his unforgiving island audience. As Chang and Chen write: "Shabba Ranks lost credibility in the eyes of the dancehall massive. 'Shabba bow' was the common view. He had given in to foreign and economic pressure and betrayed his beliefs."[94]

After the controversy blew over, however, Shabba was able to revive his career, and his greatest success came after his songs were used in Hollywood movies. In 1992 the Jamaican hit single "Mr. Loverman" was used in the film *Deep Cover*, pushing the song to number one on U.S. R&B charts. That same year, Shabba was the first dancehall deejay to win a Grammy award when his Epic debut with Maxi Priest, *Raw as Ever*, hit number one on the R&B charts. In 1994, Shabba's rap/reggae remake of the 1971 Sly and the Family Stone hit "Family Affair" was a hit after it was used in the film *Addams Family Values*.

Returning to Roots

The popularity of "Family Affair" proved that reggae sounds were still viable in the marketplace. And in the late 1990s, even as dancehall lyrics continued to glorify sex and violence, there was a renaissance of rasta music afoot in Jamaica. This split was so pronounced that music writers began dividing Jamaican music into two separate schools. The older style consisted of "bashment" artists who rapped, chanted, and toasted over hardcore dancehall rhythms about subjects such as women, guns, dance moves, and dancehall fashions. The other camp became known as "consciousness" singers. These people are described by Barrow and Dalton as "a new breed of roots and cultural proselytizers, often employing fuller rhythms that recall (or are versions of) classics from the 1970s."[95]

David "Ziggy" Marley, second son of Bob and Rita Marley, is undoubtedly the most famous singer in the consciousness camp. Sounding like a younger version of his father, Ziggy has recorded a half dozen successful albums with his siblings Cedella (named after her grandmother), Sharon, and Stephen in the Melody Makers.

While the Melody Makers blend roots reggae, rap, and blues, their music is aimed squarely at the American market and at fans of Bob Marley. In Jamaica, however, there has been a roots resurgence in the twenty-first century led by singers Sizzla, Anthony B., and Capelton. Like previous Rastafari singers, these artists rely on their faith, known as Bobo Ashanti, to inform their

Ziggy Marley has followed in his father's musical footsteps. Together with his siblings, he is part of the successful band, the Melody Makers.

Ziggy Marley and the Melody Makers

When Bob and Rita Marley's second son, Ziggy, was born in 1968, his father had yet to achieve international acclaim. However, even before Bob Marley's death in 1981, Ziggy knew he wanted to follow in his father's musical footsteps. Ziggy Marley's career is described on the Ziggymarley.com Web site:

Ziggy Marley first sat in on recording sessions with his father's band, legendary reggae troupe Bob Marley and the Wailers, when he was ten years old. Joining with his three siblings to become The Melody Makers, Ziggy crafted his own soulful sound blending blues, R&B, hip-hop and roots reggae.

After their first two albums, *Play The Game Right* (1985) and *Hey World!* (1986), The Melody Makers earned their first Grammy (Best Reggae Recording) for *Conscious Party* (1988). . . .

While selling records by the millions and selling out countless concerts with the Melody Makers, . . . Ziggy Marley has never lost sight of his foundation of faith, fellowship and family. After two decades as the driving creative force behind The Melody Makers, Ziggy stepped out on his own with his first solo album, *Dragonfly* (2003). . . . "Working on my own gave me a chance to take my time and experiment a lot," Ziggy says of the material on *Dragonfly*. . . . Although the members of the most close-knit musical families often yearn to step out on their own, for Ziggy, a solo debut was not a long-awaited goal. "It's not something that I wished for since I began doing music," he says. "It was just the circumstances, and I wanted to be true to myself and what I feel. The record has strong messages and it feels good."

music. This branch of Rastafarianism is an orthodox sect that practices what might be called fundamentalist Rastafari. Believers call men "kings," women "empresses," and children "princes" and "princesses." They adhere to strict vegetarian diets and pray often, and men wear turbans tightly wrapped around their dreadlocks. In Kingston, where violence, poverty, hopelessness, and lawlessness are worse than ever, the Bobo Ashanti message delivered by

Sizzla and others appeals because some young people demand music with a nonmaterialist message.

Like previous incarnations of reggae, the militant "Bobo-dread" message has been controversial. For example, Anthony B.'s song "Fire Pon Rome" has an anti-Catholic message that resulted in a spate of church firebombings in Jamaica. Bradley offers a rationale for the popularity of such music:

> It's this same kind of fierceness that appeals to many youths—confrontational lyrics, hardcore rhythms, in your face deliveries—and has given Bobo records a place in the dancehall. While a large fanbase may not go so far as to wear a turban, they go along with the whiff of violence involved.[96]

The rise of Bobo, which brings traditional elements of reggae into a new century, is consistent with the way Jamaican music has evolved since the days of slavery. Everything old is made new again in a musical culture where reinvention is a time-honored tradition. That so many innovative genres should emerge from a small population on a poverty-stricken Caribbean island is unprecedented in the annals of music history.

On an island where sounds of homegrown music fill the air, where people toil by day so they can dance and sing at night, the history of reggae is written in the blood of the Jamaican people.

• Notes •

Introduction: The Movement of the People

1. Lloyd Bradley, *Reggae: The Story of Jamaican Music*. London: BBC, 2002, p. 7.
2. Quoted in Lloyd Bradley, *Bass Culture: When Reggae Was King*. London: Viking, 2000, p. vii.
3. Quoted in Stephen A. King, *Reggae, Rastafari, and the Rhetoric of Social Control*. Jackson: University Press of Mississippi, 2002, p. 45.
4. Stacey Herbold, "Jamaican Patois and the Power of Language in Reggae Music," Dread Library, University of Vermont. http://debate.uvm.edu/dreadlibrary/herbold.html.
5. Quoted in Norman C. Stolzoff, *Wake the Town and Tell the People*. Durham, NC: Duke University Press, 2000, p. 3.

Chapter One: The Roots of Reggae

6. Quoted in Chris Salewicz, *Reggae Explosion: The Story of Jamaican Music*. New York: Abrams, 2001, p. 20.
7. Salewicz, *Reggae Explosion*, p.21.
8. Quoted in Nathaniel Samuel Murrell, William David Spencer, and Adrian Anthony McFarlane, eds., *Chanting Down Babylon: The Rastafari Reader*. Philadelphia: Temple University Press, 1998.

9. Quoted in Murrell, Spencer, and McFarlane, *Chanting Down Babylon*, pp. 234–35.
10. Quoted in Carter Van Pelt, "Burru Style: An Interview with Skatalites Drummer Lloyd Knibb," 1998. http://incolor.inetnebr.com/cvanpelt/knibb.html.
11. Quoted in Carter Van Pelt, "Burru Style."
12. Quoted in David Katz, *People Funny Boy*. Edinburgh, UK: Payback Press, 2000, p. 65.
13. Quoted in David Katz, *Solid Foundation: An Oral History of Reggae*. New York: Bloomsbury, 2003, p. 16.
14. Kevin O'Brien Chang and Wayne Chen, *Reggae Routes*. Philadelphia: Temple University Press, 1998, p. 14.
15. Steve Barrow and Peter Dalton, *The Rough Guide to Reggae*. London: Rough Guides, 2001, p. 7.
16. Chang and Chen, *Reggae Routes*, p. 14.
17. Quoted in Katz, *Solid Foundation*, p. 14.
18. Quoted in Katz, *Solid Foundation*, p. 16.
19. Quoted in Katz, *Solid Foundation*, p. 3.

Chapter Two: The Sounds of Sound System

20. Salewicz, *Reggae Explosion*, p. 26.

21. Quoted in Katz, *Solid Foundation*, p. 4.
22. Mohair Slim, "The Untold Story of Jamaican Popular Music," Blue Juice—Blues, Soul, Jazz and Ska, 2001. www.trinity.unimelb.edu.au/~mwilliam/bj/skareggae/Boogie.php.
23. Quoted in Barrow and Dalton, *The Rough Guide to Reggae*, p. 11.
24. Quoted in Barrow and Dalton, *The Rough Guide to Reggae*, p. 12.
25. Quoted in Barrow and Dalton, *The Rough Guide to Reggae*, p. 19.
26. Quoted in Slim, "The Untold Story of Jamaican Popular Music."
27. Quoted in Stolzoff, *Wake the Town and Tell the People*, p. 57.
28. Quoted in Katz, *People Funny Boy*, p. 7.
29. Quoted in Stolzoff, *Wake the Town and Tell the People*, pp. 56–57.
30. Barrow and Dalton, *The Rough Guide to Reggae*, p. 13.
31. Salewicz, *Reggae Explosion*, p. 27.
32. Quoted in Barrow and Dalton, *The Rough Guide to Reggae*, p. 15.
33. Quoted in Bradley, *Reggae*, p. 31.
34. Chang and Chen, *Reggae Routes*, p. 21.
35. Quoted in Chang and Chen, *Reggae Routes*, p. 21.
36. Quoted in Barrow and Dalton, *The Rough Guide to Reggae*, p. 16.
37. Katz, *Solid Foundation*, p. 3.

Chapter Three: Ska and Rocksteady

38. Bradley, *Reggae*, p. 11.
39. Slim, "The Untold Story of Jamaican Popular Music."
40. Quoted in Katz, *Solid Foundation*, p. 31.
41. Quoted in Slim, "The Untold Story of Jamaican Popular Music."
42. Bradley, *Reggae*, p. 12.
43. Quoted in Slim, "The Untold Story of Jamaican Popular Music."
44. Chris Wilson, liner notes, *Original Club Ska* compact disc. Cambridge, MA: Heartbeat Records, 1990.
45. Quoted in Chang and Chen, *Reggae Routes*, p. 32.
46. Quoted in Stolzoff, *Wake the Town and Tell the People*, p. 237.
47. Brian Keyo, liner notes, *Ska Foundation: The Skatalites* compact disc. Cambridge, MA: Heartbeat Records, 1997.
48. Quoted in Murrell, Spencer, and McFarlane, *Chanting Down Babylon*, p. 237.
49. Slim, "The Untold Story of Jamaican Popular Music."
50. Katz, *Solid Foundation*, p. 65.
51. Quoted in Chang and Chen, *Reggae Routes*, p. 39.
52. Bradley, *Reggae*, p. 38.
53. Quoted in Chang and Chen, *Reggae Routes*, p. 39.
54. Chang and Chen, *Reggae Routes*, p. 41.
55. Barrow and Dalton, *The Rough Guide to Reggae*, p. 59.

Chapter Four: Bob Marley and the Reggae Explosion

56. Quoted in Bradley, *Bass Culture*, p 203.
57. Quoted in Chang and Chen, *Reggae Routes*, p. 42.
58. Quoted in Leonard E. Barrett Sr.,

The Rastafarians. Boston: Beacon, 1997, p. 9.

59. Mikal Gilmore, "The Life and Times of Bob Marley: How He Changed the World Forever," *Rolling Stone*, March 10, 2005, p. 70.

60. Gilmore, "The Life and Times of Bob Marley," p. 71.

61. Bradley, *Bass Culture*, p. 284.

62. Timothy White, *Catch Fire: The Life of Bob Marley*. New York: Henry Holt, 1998, pp. 239–40.

63. White, *Catch Fire*, p. 261.

64. Gilmore, "The Life and Times of Bob Marley," p. 73.

65. Chang and Chen, *Reggae Routes*, p. 58.

66. Quoted in Ian McCann, *Bob Marley in His Own Words*. London: Omnibus, 1993, p. 94.

67. Quoted in McCann, *Bob Marley in His Own Words*, p. 86.

Chapter Five: Dub, Toasting, and Dancehall

68. Bradley, *Bass Culture*, p. 312.

69. Quoted in Chris Yurkiw, "Like a Version," *Montreal Mirror*, December 3, 1997. www.montrealmirror. com/AR CHIVES/1997/120497/music4.html.

70. Quoted in Yurkiw, "Like a Version."

71. Quoted in Bradley, *Bass Culture*, p. 314.

72. Quoted in Barrow and Dalton, *The Rough Guide to Reggae*, p. 227.

73. Bradley, *Bass Culture*, p. 316.

74. Katz, *Solid Foundation*, p. 294.

75. Quoted in Kwame Davis, *Natural Mysticsim: Towards a New Reggae Aesthetic*. Leeds, England: Peepal Tree Press, 1999, p. 82.

76. Quoted in Katz, *Solid Foundation*, p. 295.

77. Quoted in Chang and Chen, *Reggae Routes*, p. 59.

78. Barrow and Dalton, *The Rough Guide to Reggae*, p. 261.

79. Stolzoff, *Wake the Town and Tell the People*, pp. 109–110.

80. Quoted in Barrow and Dalton, *The Rough Guide to Reggae*, p. 273.

81. Quoted in "Eek a Mouse Biography," Eek a Mouse—the Fansite. www.angelfire.com/ak/eekamouse.

82. Bradley, *Reggae*, p. 122.

Chapter Six: Ragga and Reggae Worldwide

83. Bradley, *Reggae*, p. 131.

84. Bradley, *Reggae*, p. 133.

85. Stolzoff, *Wake the Town and Tell the People*, p. 107.

86. Maureen Sheridan, "Dancehall Courts Danger," *Billboard*, November 13, 1993, p. 46.

87. Quoted in Sheridan, "Dancehall Courts Danger," p. 46.

88. Ben Thielen, "The Change of Messages in Dancehall," Dread Library, University of Vermont. http://debate. uvm.edu/ dreadlibrary/thielen.html.

89. Quoted in Basil Walters, "Celebrating Women in Reggae," *Jamaica Observer*, May 17, 2004. www.ja maicaobserver.com/magazines/All Woman/html/20040517T020000 0500_59975_OBS_CELEBRATING _WOMEN_IN_REGGAE.asp.

90. Barrow and Dalton, *The Rough Guide to Reggae*, p. 327.
91. Quoted in Barrow and Dalton, *The Rough Guide to Reggae*, p. 327.
92. Quoted in Bradley, *Reggae*, p. 140.
93. mp3.com, "Cocoa Tea," 2005. www.mp3.com/CocoaTea/artists/24476/biography.html.
94. Chang and Chen, *Reggae Routes*, p. 204.
95. Barrow and Dalton, *The Rough Guide to Reggae*, p. 363.
96. Bradley, *Reggae*, p. 148.

• For Further Reading •

Books

Lloyd Bradley, *Reggae: The Story of Jamaican Music*. London: BBC, 2002. A book written to accompany the British Broadcasting Company's television series on reggae, which was produced to commemorate the fortieth anniversary of Jamaican independence from Great Britain.

Bob Brunning, *Reggae*. New York: Peter Bedrick, 1999. Highlights some of the most influential stars on the reggae scene, including Aswad, Dennis Brown, Burning Spear, Prince Buster, and Bob Marley.

James Haskins, *One Love, One Heart*. New York: Jump at the Sun, 2003. A history of reggae for young adults that focuses on how the music has helped shape the culture, religion, dress, and language of Jamaica.

Bruce W. Talamon and Roger Steffens, *Bob Marley: Spirit Dancer*. New York: W.W. Norton, 1994. Dozens of photographs of Bob Marley during the last two years of his life, accompanied by text that explains the photographs and provides biographical information.

Web Sites

The Dread Library (http://debate.uvm.edu/dreadlibrary/dreadlibrary.html). Links to dozens of articles concerning reggae history, Rastafarianism, Bob Marley, women in reggae, the style's African influences, dub, dancehall, and more.

Jammin' Reggae Archives (http://niceup.com/index.html). Artist biographies, reggae sounds, tour dates, periodicals, mp3 downloads, and virtual radio links are available on this comprehensive site dedicated to Jamaican music.

Ska/Reggae (www.trinity.unimelb.edu.au/~mwilliam/bj/skareggae). An informative Web site created by Mohair Slim, deejay on the PBS radio show *Blue Juice*. The site includes links to pages with reggae history, interviews with reggae legends, Jamaican chart hits since the 1960s, and a patois dictionary.

• Works Consulted •

Books

Leonard E. Barrett Sr., *The Rastafarians.* Boston: Beacon, 1997. The beliefs, dynamics, rituals, music, and art of Jamaica's unique religion, which developed in the context of colonial exploitation and grinding poverty.

Steve Barrow and Peter Dalton, *The Rough Guide to Reggae.* London: Rough Guides, 2001. A compendium of reggae music that covers the entire span of recorded music in Jamaica from the 1950s mento through R&B, dancehall, dub, ragga, reggae, and more.

Lloyd Bradley, *Bass Culture: When Reggae Was King.* London: Viking, 2000. A history of reggae from its origins in Jamaican sound-system dances of the 1950s, through its enormous international popularity in the 1970s, to the current generation of new artists.

Kevin O'Brien Chang and Wayne Chen, *Reggae Routes.* Philadelphia: Temple University Press, 1998. The story of Jamaican music portrayed as the nation's main emotional outlet and chief cultural contribution to the world.

Kwame Davis, *Natural Mysticism: Towards a New Reggae Aesthetic.* Leeds, England: Peepal Tree Press, 1999. A work of Jamaican cultural analysis that ties the lyrical, melodic, and rhythmic elements of reggae to political, spiritual, and societal forces of change throughout the world.

Stephen Davis, *Bob Marley.* Rochester, VT: Shenkman, 1990. A biography of reggae's most renowned singer-songwriter, relating the story of his rise from the slums to the heights of international stardom.

———, *Reggae Bloodlines.* Garden City, NY: Anchor, 1979. A book that explores the more controversial political aspects of reggae music as it is used to protest government policies and living conditions for the poor in Jamaica.

David Katz, *People Funny Boy.* Edinburgh, UK: Payback, 2000. A biography of self-described lunatic Lee "Scratch" Perry, one of Jamaica's most colorful singer/producer/songwriters.

———, *Solid Foundation: An Oral History of Reggae.* New York: Bloomsbury, 2003. A series of conversations with the architects of Jamaican reggae music, including Jimmy Cliff, Toots and the Maytals, the Wailers, Gregory Isaacs, Burning Spear, and many more.

Stephen A. King, *Reggae, Rastafari, and the Rhetoric of Social Control.* Jackson: University Press of Mississippi, 2002. The history of Rastafarian musical protest in ska, rocksteady, rude boy, reggae, and other Jamaican music.

Rita Marley and Hettie Jones, *No Woman No Cry*. New York: Hyperion, 2004. The autobiography of the woman who married Bob Marley in 1966, sang with him in his band the Wailers, and continues to perform with the reggae group the I-Threes.

Ian McCann, *Bob Marley in His Own Words*. London: Omnibus, 1993. The reggae superstar discusses his early days, music, politics, religion, stardom, and other aspects of his life. Compiled from various interviews Marley gave over the years.

Nathaniel Samuel Murrell, William David Spencer, and Adrian Anthony McFarlane, eds., *Chanting Down Babylon: The Rastafari Reader*. Philadelphia: Temple University Press, 1998. A series of articles written by scholars about Rastafarian ideology, culture, history, arts, music, and theology.

Chris Salewicz, *Reggae Explosion: The Story of Jamaican Music*. New York: Abrams, 2001. A large, colorful book, with dozens of striking photographs, that provides an informed and insightful history of reggae music and its roots in Jamaican culture.

Norman C. Stolzoff, *Wake the Town and Tell the People*. Durham, NC: Duke University Press, 2000. A study of dancehall culture in Jamaica that goes beyond the music to explore the history, politics, and sociological characteristics that influence nearly every aspect of Kingston ghetto life.

Timothy White, *Catch Fire: The Life of Bob Marley*. New York: Henry Holt, 1998. First published in 1983, this definitive history of Marley's life delves into the intrigues of the reggae music business, offers a sweeping social history of modern Jamaica, and explores the origins of the Rastafarian religion.

Internet Sources

"Cocoa Tea," mp3.com, 2005. www.mp3. com/Cocoa-Tea/artists/24476/biog raphy.html.

"Eek a Mouse Biography," Eek a Mouse —the Fansite. www.angelfire. com/ ak/eekamouse.

Stacey Herbold, "Jamaican Patois and the Power of Language in Reggae Music," Dread Library, University of Vermont. http://debate.uvm.edu/ dreadlibrary/herbold.html.

Mohair Slim, "The Untold Story of Jamaican Popular Music," Blue Juice —Blues, Soul, Jazz and Ska, 2001. www.trinity.unimelb.edu.au/~mwill iam/bj/skareggae/Boogie.php.

Ben Thielen, "The Change of Messages in Dancehall," Dread Library University of Vermont. http://debate. uvm.edu/dreadlibrary/thielen.html.

Carter Van Pelt, "Burru Style: An Interview with Skatalites Drummer Lloyd Knibb," 1998. http://incolor. inetnebr.com/cvanpelt/knibb.html.

Basil Walters, "Celebrating Women in Reggae," *Jamaica Observer*, May 17, 2004. www.jamaicaobserver.com/

magmagazines/AllWoman/html/20 040517T0200000500_59975_OBS _CELEBRATING_WOMEN_IN_ REGGAE.asp.

Chris Yurkiw, "Like a Version," *Montreal Mirror*, December 3, 1997. www.montrealmirror.com/ARCHI VES/1997/120497/music4.html.

Periodicals

Mikal Gilmore, "The Life and Times of Bob Marley: How He Changed the World Forever," *Rolling Stone*, March 10, 2005. An article about the reggae superstar and his influence on popular music.

Maureen Sheridan, "Dancehall Courts Danger," *Billboard*, November 13, 1993. An article about the increased violence in Jamaica as reflected in the gun songs popular in dancehalls in the 1990s.

Other Sources

Ted Bafaloukos, director, *Rockers*, Music Video Distribution, March 14, 2000. A DVD release of the 1978 film made during reggae's heyday, featuring major players Burning Spear, Big Youth, Jacob Miller, the Heptones, the Mighty Diamonds, Gregory Isaacs, and others.

Brian Keyo, liner notes, *Ska Foundation: The Skatalites*. compact disc. Cambridge, MA: Heartbeat Records, 1997. The history of the Skatalites, the founding fathers of Jamaica's original sound.

Chris Wilson, liner notes, *Original Club Ska*. compact disc. Cambridge, MA: Heartbeat Records, 1990. A short history of ska music included with a CD of some early dancehall hits.

• Index •

• Picture Credits •

• About the Author •

Stuart A. Kallen is the author of more than two hundred nonfiction books for children and young adults. He has written on topics ranging from the theory of relativity to the history of rock and roll. In addition, Mr. Kallen has written award-winning children's videos and television scripts. In his spare time, Stuart A. Kallen is a singer/songwriter/guitarist in San Diego, California.